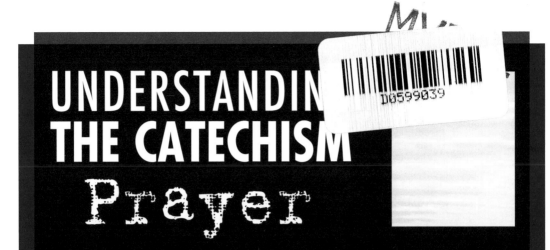

UNDERSTANDING THE CATECHISM
Prayer

THOMAS RUHLAND

RCL Benziger

Cincinnati, Ohio

> "The Ad Hoc Committee to Oversee
> the Use of the Catechism,
> National Conference of Catholic Bishops,
> has found this catechetical text
> to be in conformity with
> the *Catechism of the Catholic Church*."

To my lifemate Katherine Mary;
To the miracles that I have had the honor
    of fathering, Anna Marie and Noah Thomas;
In memory of our son David Thomas
    and of my father Melvin Peter.
To my mother Elaine who cultivated
    the seeds of faith in me;
And in thanksgiving to Margaret Reif,
    my teacher and writing mentor.

Author: Thomas Ruhland

Product Manager: Mike Carotta
Senior Editor: Ron Lamping
Project Editor: Karen Griffith
Senior Production Editor: Laura Fremder

Art Director: Pat Bracken
Page Design: Dennis Davidson
Production Manager: Jenna Nelson
Cover Design: Pat Bracken

NIHIL OBSTAT
Rev. Msgr. Glenn D. Gardner, J.C.D.
Censor Librorum

IMPRIMATUR
† Most Rev. Charles V. Grahmann
Bishop of Dallas

June 8, 1998

The Nihil Obstat and Imprimatur are official declarations
that the material reviewed is free of doctrinal or moral
error. No implication is contained therein that those
granting the Nihil Obstat and Imprimatur agree with
the contents, opinions, or statements expressed.

ACKNOWLEDGMENTS

Scripture selections are taken from the *New American
Bible* © 1991, 1986, 1970 by the Confraternity of
Christian Doctrine, Washington, D.C. and are used
by license of the copyright owner. All rights reserved.
No part of the New American Bible may be used or
reproduced in any form, without the permission of the
copyright owner.

Excerpts from the English translation of the *Catechism
of the Catholic Church* for the United States of America
copyright © 1994 United States Catholic Conference,
Inc.—Libreria Editrice Vaticana. Used with permission.

Excerpts from *Vatican Council II: The Conciliar and
Post Conciliar Documents, New Revised Edition,* Austin
Flannery, O.P., Gen. Ed. Copyright © 1975, 1986, 1992,
1996 by Costello Publishing Company, Inc. Used by
permission. Excerpts from *Catholic Household Blessings
and Prayers* (revised edition) © 2007, United States
Conference of Catholic Bishops, Washington, D.C.

Photos: Art Resource, 25, 73; Barnzin/
FPG International, 66; Robert Paul Conklin/Uniphoto,
100; Jim Cummins/FPG International, 6; Daemmrich/
Tony Stone Images, 76; Dennis Full, 51, 112; NASA, 16;
Bill Stanton/International Stock, 105; SuperStock, 28,
54; Arthur Tilley/FPG International, 18.

Send all inquiries to:
RCL Benziger
8805 Governor's Hill Drive • Suite 400
Cincinnati, Ohio 45249

Toll Free   877-275-4725
Fax   800-688-8356

Visit us at www.RCLBenziger.com

Printed in the United States of America

20256   ISBN 978-0-7829-0878-7 (Student Book)
20257   ISBN 978-0-7829-0879-4 (Teacher's Guide)

9th Printing.
January 2014.

Contents

Introduction

The Seeds We Sow

This book on prayer will draw upon the richness of the *Catechism of the Catholic Church* as it uncovers the awesome mystery of our God whom we come to know more deeply through an active prayer life. It will uncover and help to break open the profound ideas and teachings on prayer that are held within our Catholic Tradition. It is the goal of this text that you will find your journey into prayer to be satisfying and rewarding.

Exploring and developing a Christian spirituality is also challenging, often difficult, and sometimes painful. The up side is that this struggle ultimately draws us closer to who we really are. Our identity is in our Creator God. As the Book of Genesis tells us,

"God created man in his image;
in the divine image he created him;
male and female he created them"
(Genesis 1:27).

Here the roots of our existence are laid bare and it is here that we discover life's deepest meanings.

"A sower went out to sow. And as he sowed, some seed fell on the path, and birds came and ate it up. . . . But some seed fell on rich soil, and produced fruit, a hundred or sixty or thirtyfold."

Matthew 13:3–4, 8

CHAPTER 1

Cultivating the Soil

Rejoice in the Lord always. . . . The Lord is near.
Have no anxiety at all, but in everything,
by prayer and petition, with thanksgiving,
make your requests known to God.

PHILIPPIANS 4:4–6

What Do You Think?

Write "T" or "F" beside each of the following to indicate whether you think the statement is true or false.

_____ 1. Prayer is easy; all you have to do is bring a list to God.

_____ 2. When I pray, God listens and answers me.

_____ 3. People pray for different purposes.

_____ 4. Praying will change your life.

_____ 5. Christians can get close to God without prayer.

Share the reasons for your choices.

Like many students, Thomas was raised a Catholic. He went to a Catholic school, was an altar server, and said the routine prayers each day at meals and at bedtime with his family. But now he is in high school, and things are changing: his hair style, his music. Thomas also realizes that his prayer is changing; he begins to realize that God is more than someone you believe about, but rather someone you believe in. He is concerned that his faith isn't his own, but is the faith of his parents!

Then one night at the parish youth group, something happened. Liz, the youth minister, reminded Thomas of something. "God really loves you," she said. "And not only that, God wants to have a relationship with you, just like you want a relationship with some of your friends. All you have to do is say yes and accept the invitation of God's friendship."

Looking back, that night became one of the most important moments in Thomas's life. It was then that Thomas made the choice to enter into a relationship with God, and that choice has affected and will affect all the rest of the choices in his life.

KEY TERMS

covenant

humility

prayer

spirituality

How would you describe your relationship with God?

Thomas began to realize that **prayer, spirituality,** and the gift of faith are at the heart of his life. Spirituality is every bit a part of the human experience as are the dimensions of psychology, sociability, intelligence, sexuality, morality, and emotions. A healthy and meaningful prayer and spiritual life is cultivated carefully out of the soil of our lives and, if tended to properly, will yield a fruitful harvest. In this chapter we begin to break open the ideas and beliefs about prayer that are put forth in the *Catechism of the Catholic Church.*

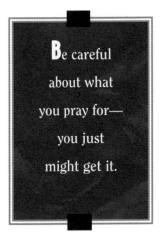

Be careful about what you pray for— you just might get it.

(*Catechism of the Catholic Church*, 2559–2565)

What Is Prayer?

Prayer is serious business. It is God's invitation to us to talk and listen to him. More than anything else, prayer is transformational. It will change our lives.

Saint Thérèse of Lisieux (Thérèse of the Child Jesus) wrote, "For me, prayer is a surge of the heart; it is a simple look, turned toward heaven, it is a cry of recognition and of love, embracing both trial and joy."

Saint Thérèse touches on the paradoxical nature of a prayerful life. It is at the same time simple and complex. Prayer is as simple as a "turn toward heaven," but it also embraces both "trial and joy."

As human beings we are a unique creation. We see life from a variety of perspectives. We look at life through many different "lenses" that help us understand reality. We attempt to find answers to life's most complicated, gut-churning questions about the purpose of life, God, love, and meaning. These are the questions that seem to drive us deeper into the roots of existence.

Those who have faced suffering and pain, through the loss of a loved one or a relationship that has broken up, have asked questions about the purpose of their lives. "Why?" we ask. "Why did *my* son die?" "Why did *my* father contract cancer?" "Why do people suffer at all?" "What kind of a God makes, or even allows, bad things to happen to people, especially good people?"

We ask these "ultimate" questions, and the answers, if they have any meaning for us, do not come easily. It is within this context of our lives that God reveals his constant, caring presence.

Recognizing God in the Ordinary

We often look for God in the extraordinary events of human life. We busy ourselves with this notion so much that we fail to recognize God in the ordinary events of our daily life. God is a God of the ordinary experiences, like a sunrise or a rainfall, or the winter's first snowstorm.

Prayer Questionnaire

1. How do you know that God exists?

2. What is prayer?

3. Why do we pray?

4. Why does it seem that God answers some people's prayers and not others?

5. When we pray for someone who is sick and they do not get well, is God trying to tell us something about life? About the nature and purpose of prayer? About the nature of God?

6. Prayer, it is said, draws us closer to God. How do you think this happens?

7. In what times of your life do you seem to pray the most?

8. What prayers have you learned that you seem to come back to in times of need or stress? What is it about these particular prayers that you find comforting?

9. When was the last time you prayed? What was the reason? Did it help your situation?

10. Saint Ignatius says that "just the *desire* to get closer to God draws us closer to God." Describe what this desire is like for you.

Praying is like that too. Praying is not only saying the Hail Mary, or reciting the Rosary, or going to Mass. It is looking for God in the people around you: in your friends, parents, siblings, other students, and teachers; in the ordinary events that make up your day.

Prayer is forced silence—taking the time to quiet yourself amidst the clutter of the day and slowing down to listen to God's voice in your life. Prayer is being in love with God and experiencing your heart's deepest desire to be one with the object of your affections.

Faith can be described as trusting God with all your heart. Prayer is the fuel for a mature and vibrant faith life. Prayer is the intimate communication between God and humans. In the book *Old Turtle* by Douglas Woods (1993), the Old Turtle says that people "are a message of love from God to the earth, and a prayer from the earth back to God."

(CCC, 2559)

Prayer as God's Gift

Humility is one of the virtues that we seem to have little grasp of in our modern culture. Perhaps there is an arrogance in Western culture that has come about as a result of our ever-increasing knowledge of the world. We have acquired more scientific knowledge in the past fifty years than in all the time before that period combined. We seem to have "figured out" what we used to call mysterious questions.

Scientific inquiry has brought us to the threshold of truth—or so we think.

One night a man had a dream. He dreamed he was walking along the beach with the Lord.

Across the sky flashed scenes from his life; for each scene he noticed two sets of footprints in the sand—one belonged to him and the other to the Lord.

When the last scene of his life flashed before him he looked back at the footprints in the sand. He noticed that, many times, along the path of his life, there was only one set of footprints. He also noticed that it happened to be at the very lowest and saddest times of his life. This really bothered him, and he questioned the Lord about it.

"Lord, you said that once I decided to follow you, you'd walk with me all the way. But I noticed that during the most troublesome times of my life there was only one set of footprints. I don't understand why, when I needed you most, you would leave me."

The Lord replied, "My precious, precious child. I love you and would never leave you. During your times of trials and suffering, when you see only one set of footprints, it was then that I carried you."   ANONYMOUS

.... Reflection Questions:

1. What feelings or thoughts came into your mind as you read and reflected on this story? What insight did it give you into your own experience of God?

2. Recall a time in your life when you felt God was not present or was completely absent in your life. Describe what that feeling was like.

3. At what times have you felt the presence of God most in your life? How did you respond?

No longer do we have a sense of—or even value—the "mysterious" or even the "sacred." What used to be understood in theological and spiritual terms we think now can be explained by Doppler radar. "Who needs God anymore?" some ask.

Humility comes from trust in God. It includes the realization—and conviction—that you and I don't have all the answers. Life involves mystery. For some, that realization grows out of our gut when we acknowledge that some questions are too big to be scientifically addressed, and we acknowledge God. At that point we learn humility. We acknowledge that we aren't at the center of the universe.

The Judeo-Christian tradition believes that life is a gift. Prayer is a gift. God is the giver. God creates human beings in his image just because God wants to. We inherit the sacred and are part of a profound mystery. Each of us is invited to live this awesome mystery we call human life. It is a gift, a marvelous gift.

Prayer as Covenant

We are inextricably entwined to God in a loving relationship that God initiates and we are invited to freely respond to. This is the **covenant** that God offers us. It is his unending presence in the midst of our lives. It is a presence that we are made aware of in the depths of our hearts.

God's Covenant with us unites us with God in Christ. Through Baptism we are united in Christ with the Father and the Holy Spirit. Our prayer flows from this covenant.

> Christian prayer is a covenant relationship between God and man in Christ. It is the action of God and of man, springing forth from both the Holy Spirit and ourselves.
>
> CCC, 2564

Prayer as Communion

A student, after completing a course on prayer, remarked to the teacher, "I never really got into this class; you never taught us anything 'radical.' You taught us what the Church teaches. It was nothing new, not like what science offers us."

The teacher listened carefully and responded, "What is more radical? To believe in a God who loves you and is intensely in love with you or to put all your marbles into the baskets of contemporary scientific theories? In other words, what is more transforming in someone's life, being loved, or black holes?"

It has been said that there is a God-shaped hole in every person. Only God can fill that hole. Many try to cover it or load it with all sorts of stuff, like drugs, alcohol, sex, material things, temporary relationships, and money. Try as we may, only God can fill it—nothing less. Prayer is our response to our longing for that deepest part of ourselves to be fulfilled. It is a response to God, who longs for us to know and love him.

> In the New Covenant, prayer is the living relationship of the children of God with their Father who is good beyond measure, with his Son Jesus Christ and with the Holy Spirit.
>
> CCC, 2565

We believe in this communion of life with the Holy Trinity. In Baptism we are united with Christ and his Body, the Church; we receive the gift of the Spirit and new life as adopted children of God.

Read and reflect on this prayer of Paul for the Christians living in Ephesus.

For this reason I kneel before the Father, from whom every family in heaven and on earth is named, that he may grant you in accord with the riches of his glory to be strengthened with power through his Spirit in the inner self, and that Christ may dwell in your hearts through faith; that you, rooted and grounded in love, may have strength to comprehend with all the holy ones what is the breadth and length and height and depth, and to know the love of Christ that surpasses knowledge, so that you may be filled with all the fullness of God.

Now to him who is able to accomplish far more than all we ask or imagine, by the power at work within us, to him be glory in the church and in Christ Jesus to all generations, forever and ever. Amen.

Ephesians 3:14–21

· · · · Discuss:

What does Paul's prayer say regarding prayer? About our communion with God and God's presence with us?

Prayer

❖ ❖ ❖

Praise the LORD, who is so good;
   God's love endures forever;

Praise the God of gods;
   God's love endures forever;

Praise the Lord of lords;
   God's love endures forever;

Who alone has done great
   wonders,
   God's love endures forever;

Who skillfully made the heavens,
   God's love endures forever;

Who spread the earth upon the
   waters,
   God's love endures forever;

Who made the great lights,
   God's love endures forever;

The sun to rule the day,
   God's love endures forever;

The moon and stars to rule the
   night,
   God's love endures forever.

Psalm 136:1–9

REVIEW

IMPORTANT TERMS TO KNOW

covenant—the agreement between God and people first revealed in the Old Testament and fulfilled in Jesus Christ, the New Covenant

humility—a virtue that disposes us to see ourselves honestly in relationship to God and others that leads us to praise God and live our lives according to the will of God

prayer—the living relationship of the children of God with their Father, who is good beyond measure; it is "the raising of one's mind and heart to God or the requesting of good things from God."

spirituality—the daily lived expression of our faith; Christian spirituality takes many forms, but all forms express in some way our life in Christ and the Holy Spirit.

CHAPTER SUMMARY

Saint John Damascene described prayer as "the raising of one's mind and heart to God or the requesting of good things from God." In this chapter we learned:

1. Prayer is an expression of our belief that we live in a "vital and personal relationship with the living and true God" (CCC, 2558).

2. Prayer is God's gift to us and our response to God, who invites us to share in his life and love.

3. Humility is the foundation of a life of prayer. It recognizes that life is both sacred and a mystery.

4. Prayer is an expression of our belief that we live in a covenant relationship with God. "Christian prayer is a covenant relationship between God and man in Christ" (CCC, 2564).

5. Prayer is an expression of our belief that we are children of God, living in communion with the Holy Trinity.

EXPLORING OUR CATHOLIC FAITH

1. Listening to God's Word

Jesus taught his listeners about prayer. Read and reflect on Matthew 6:5–8. What does this passage tell you about prayer?

2. Understanding the Teachings of the Catholic Church

Prayer has been described as "the raising of one's mind and heart to God or the requesting of good things from God." Beginning with this teaching of the Church about the nature of prayer, write a brief paragraph about prayer. Include prayer as gift, communion, and covenant.

3. Reflecting on Our Catholic Faith

Reflect on this insight into prayer: "If the heart is far from God, the words of prayer are in vain." How might this insight apply to your prayer life? Write your thoughts in your journal.

4. Living Our Catholic Faith

Prayer has been described as "forced silence—taking the time to quiet yourself amidst the clutter of the day." Discuss with others the value of "forced silence." Draw up a plan of "forced silence" and put it into action.

CHAPTER 2

The Revelation of Prayer: Our Yearning for God

O LORD, our Lord,
>   how awesome is your name through all
>   the earth!
>   You have set your majesty above
>   the heavens!   PSALM 8:2

In the space provided write whether you agree or disagree with this statement: *Belief in God changes a person's outlook on life.* Give reasons for your response.

KEY TERMS

Covenant of Sinai

Diaspora

Hebrews

hesed

People of God

prophets

Revelation

Sacred Tradition

Look what I did, Momma! Before, all Piedro could do was swim around in his fishbowl. So I built an underwater highway in the fishbowl."

Manuel tried to get the fish to swim through the tunnel and down the road. "Hey, Piedro, why don't you swim through the tunnel and down the road?" he would ask over and over again. "That is why I made them for you." But there was no response.

Manuel's mother watched and listened. She looked into his brown eyes and saw how unhappy he was. "Manuel," she finally said, "the problem is you don't speak the same language as the fish." There was a silence. Manuel went back to the bowl on the table and wished he could become a fish.

What parallels can you find between this story and God's relationship with us?

Manuel wished he could communicate with his fish. From our Catholic perspective this story can serve to illustrate the mystery of the love of God for human beings. God created people and invites us to enter into relationship with him. This chapter will address ways that our ancestors, the **Hebrews,** listened to and responded to God's invitation to enter into the covenant relationship with him.

(*Catechism of the Catholic Church,* 2566–2567)

The Universal Call to Prayer

We are in search of God, who calls us to himself in love and kindness. God reveals his presence to us in an intimate relationship. Prayer is an expression of that relationship.

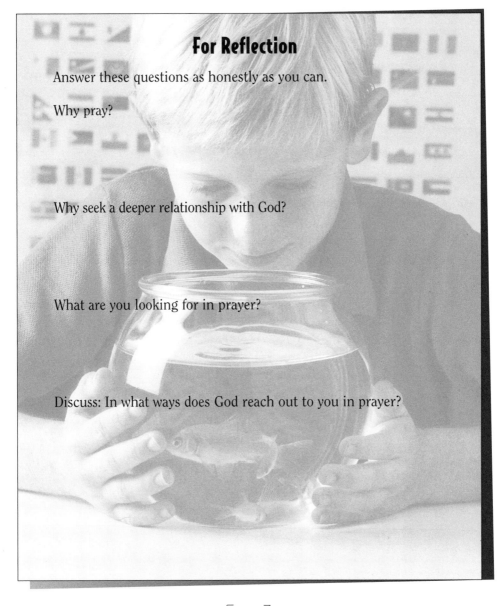

For Reflection

Answer these questions as honestly as you can.

Why pray?

Why seek a deeper relationship with God?

What are you looking for in prayer?

Discuss: In what ways does God reach out to you in prayer?

[T]he living and true God tirelessly calls each person to that mysterious encounter known as prayer. In prayer, the faithful God's initiative of love always comes first; our own first step is always a response.

CCC, 2567

Christian prayer has its origin in the peoples of the Old Testament. In their unique and uncommon relationship with God lie the roots of our Christian faith, our prayer, our life.

The **Sacred Tradition** of the Catholic Church echoes the wisdom of the past. It helps us understand our present in order to move forward into the future of our faith. It is important to listen to those who went before us, as they have much to teach us about the nature of prayer and the faith-filled life.

From our roots in Hebrew history we discover our identity as the **People of God.** After all, we are made in the image of God—we have a spiritual dimension that only finds completeness in God. Our search for God is written into our human nature. Our search for God is the fulfillment of our humanness. The search is marked with a hunger for God, who calls us to prayer—to the heart of himself where we are transformed and made new.

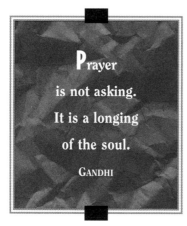

Prayer
is not asking.
It is a longing
of the soul.

GANDHI

For Reflection:

How often do you pray? (Each day? Each week?)

When was the last time you prayed?

What was it that you prayed about?

How have you experienced the presence of God when you prayed? Describe it.

Our Ancestors' Experience of God through Prayer

Even in the grandeur of perfect surroundings the first human beings were not satisfied. Because they were free to reject God, they separated themselves from him. But God did not abandon us. The Old Testament is the **Revelation** of God's initiative through people like Abraham, Moses, Solomon and the **prophets,** to reconnect, to reestablish a relationship between himself and humankind.

Journal Writing:

Complete the sentence.
"In creation, I have experienced the presence of God . . . "

This relationship was solidified in the **Covenant of Sinai** through which God chose the Hebrew people as his own. That covenant relationship is reflected in the people's obedience, out of their love of God.

Praise the LORD from the heavens;
    give praise in the heights.
Praise him, all you angels;
    give praise, all you hosts.
Praise him, sun and moon;
    give praise, all shining stars.
Praise him, highest heavens,
    you waters above the heavens.
Let them all praise the LORD's name;
    for the LORD commanded and
    they were created.

Psalm 148:1–5

Creation

Prayer is the window from which we look to the wonder that God has bestowed on all of creation. In creation we are able to gain a deeper understanding of the truth about God. God has painted a glimpse of himself into the landscape of nature and we gaze upon it with wonder and awe.

The Old Testament reveals to us the origins of our Christian faith in the lives, questions, and experiences of the people of Israel, the Hebrews. The Israelites came to believe, in spite of all the temptations of the cultural influences of the time, in one God who would eventually reveal himself as Yahweh. They would experience a relationship so intimate, so loving and caring, that it would forever change their destiny as a people and a culture.

When we read the psalms we are introduced to the struggle, the joy, and the hope of the people of Israel. We listen and hear about their discovery of God inviting them to himself through creation. These songs give us a clear picture of the prayerful attempts of our ancestors to engage in a conversation with the Creator and deepen their love of God through that communication. Prayer draws us to God.

Abraham

While our hunger for God builds up from the depths of our soul, it is God who reaches to humankind in order to love and connect with us. This is clearly revealed to us in the story of Abraham.

The Old Testament tells us of the extraordinary relationship between God and his people. The God who revealed himself to the Hebrews is most fully revealed in Jesus Christ. We are inextricably entwined with the faith of our Israelite ancestors. Jesus was a Jew. He lived, learned, taught, suffered, and died within a Jewish context.

. . . . . The Prayer of Faith. . . . .

If we look back into the history of the Israelites we find a people with a deep willingness to do as God willed. Abraham believed that God was present to him always and had a bond with him. Abraham went forth "as the LORD directed him" (Genesis 12:4) as he surrendered to the will of God. Abraham's was a simple faith. It was a faith that would be tested against Abraham's love of his son, Isaac, and would save Isaac because of the love that Abraham had for God.

What Do You Think?

It has been said that prayer is a submission to the will of God. Another word for submission is *surrender*.

What images come to mind when you think of the word *surrender?*

Do these images help you describe your experience of prayer? Why or why not?

Moses

When Moses was tending the flock of his father-in-law Jethro, he had his first encounter with God through a burning bush. This would be a new beginning for the entire Hebrew people. Upon seeing the bush Moses moved closer to it. Whereupon God spoke to him, telling him, " 'Remove the sandals from your feet, for the place where you stand is holy ground. I am the God of your father,' he continued, 'the God of Abraham, the God of Isaac, the God of Jacob' " (Exodus 3:5–6).

The Covenant at Sinai sealed a special relationship between God and his people. The Law became the glue that bound the daily life of the people to God. Adhering to the Laws of God was a delight to those who followed them and it became the manner in which they were to express their love of God. God keeps his promises; and through a devotion to the law and a life lived in obedience to God, the Hebrews found a richness in their life.

. . . The Prayer of Intercession . . .

Moses grew to know and trust God as faithful and true. Moses drew strength from this faith and he became the mediator, or intercessor, between God and his people. He was the trusted liaison, or messenger, between the infinite God and the Hebrew people wandering in the desert.

Moses made a total of eight trips up Mount Horeb to bring the concerns of the people to God. "The prayer of Moses responds to the living God's initiative for the salvation of his people" (CCC, 2593).

The Hebrews were on a long, arduous journey to the Promised Land. It would take forty years to accomplish the goal. Imagine following a man who claims to have seen God, a man whose physical appearance changes each time he descends from the mountain where he has met with God.

The Scripture tells us, "The LORD used to speak to Moses face to face, as one man speaks to another" (Exodus 33:11). Through it all Moses remained faithful to his mission, his promise to God to deliver his chosen people to the Land of Canaan. Throughout the process, God revealed himself to the people in order to save them, to bring them back to himself in order that they might live life to the fullest.

Our own prayer is often the result of our desire to meet our needs as people. The Old Testament reassures us that God listens to us because he is a God of love who is deeply concerned with the welfare of his people.

Moses models for us a posture of prayer that is one of both trusting obedience and trusting presentation of the needs of his people to God. The prayer of Moses also foreshadows the great Mediator, Jesus.

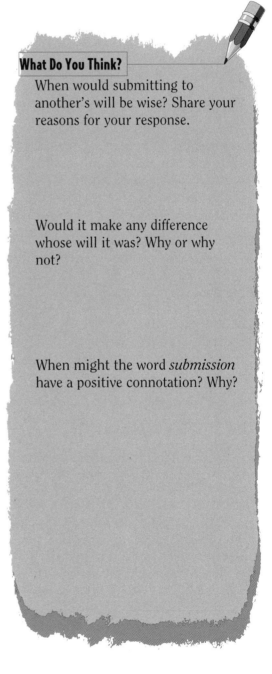

What Do You Think?

When would submitting to another's will be wise? Share your reasons for your response.

Would it make any difference whose will it was? Why or why not?

When might the word *submission* have a positive connotation? Why?

David

We are not alone in our spiritual journey. We belong to a community of believers with whom we seek to find a deep and meaningful relationship with God. In this common pursuit the prayer of David "is a faithful adherence to the divine promise and expresses a loving and joyful trust in God, the only King and Lord" (CCC, 2579).

The story of the great King David reflects yet another model of prayer for us. The king prays not only on his own behalf, but also on behalf of the entire people. He is the shepherd king who "prays for his people and prays in their name" (CCC, 2579).

The Prayer of
. . . . . the People of God . . . . .

Faith in God is more than a personal invitation from and a personal response to God. The response also is made within the context of a believing community. It is in that faith community, the community of the People of God, that our faith and our prayer are tested, challenged, and shaped in an honest and meaningful way. The Israelites clearly expressed their belief in this communal dimension of prayer. The Ark of the Covenant and the Temple of Jerusalem witness to the trust that was present among God's people.

Many people today believe that they can have a relationship with God without the benefit of a church or a faith community. We believe that God calls us to live within the community of the People of God. We grow in our faith within the heart of our tradition, a tradition that reflects the wisdom of people of faith who have made the journey and who serve to act as examples to us of the graced life of the believer.

What Do You Think?

What can other people teach us about spirituality?

Discuss: The spiritual life includes not only my relationship with God, but also my relationship with others.

Elijah

After the rule of David and the building of the Temple of Jerusalem by Solomon, his son, the Temple became a place for education in prayer and faith in the Lord. Whether in the form of pilgrimages, feasts and sacrifices, or evening offerings—all of which were signs of the holiness of God—the Hebrew people found a sacred presence in these rituals. They became a manner in which to come to worship their God more fully. To the people of that day, these were all forms of prayer. The sacred rituals that the People of God used were tools to help them understand the Awesome Mystery on which they had come to love and rely.

. . . The Prayer of Conversion . . .

Unfortunately, as in our experience today, the living of their faith was often reduced to ritual action—to the written prescriptions and externals of the ceremonies. Religion, for many, became little more than following a set of rules and regulations rather than a genuine response to the love of God in daily living. Eventually, too many of the Israelites became void of an inner spiritual life. It was during these times that the prophets, the spokespersons for God, called the People of God back to the heart of the Covenant, to the love of God and one another. Often it was the role of the prophet to stand alone, trumpeting the voice of God to "return to the LORD" (Hosea 14:3).

The voice of the prophet was constant and unwavering. It was a clear reminder of the Covenant God made with the people—a covenant that God would always remain faithful in his love for his people. The Hebrews have a word that closely describes this love of God, **hesed.** The word *hesed* means "love," "mercy," or "steadfast kindness." The prophet challenged and invited the people to return to the relationship with God. It was a call to a conversion of the heart.

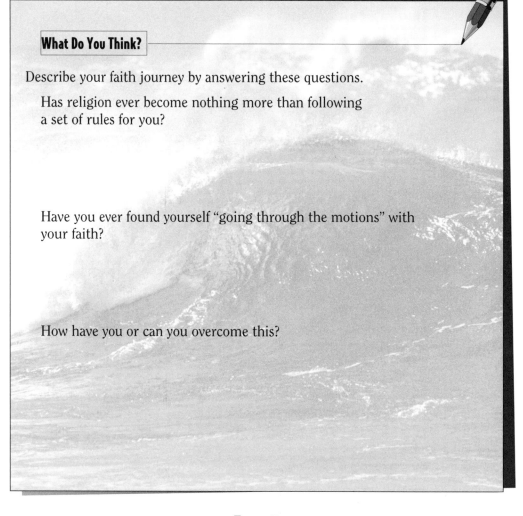

What Do You Think?

Describe your faith journey by answering these questions.

Has religion ever become nothing more than following a set of rules for you?

Have you ever found yourself "going through the motions" with your faith?

How have you or can you overcome this?

The Psalmist

The Book of Psalms is a beautiful collection of songs of prayer used in the Hebrew community in various settings of worship. It is considered the "masterwork of prayer" in the Old Testament. The psalms were the prayers that flowed from the heart of the People of God. They expressed their deepest longings, their love and praise, their sorrow and emptiness. They were rooted in the Israelite faith in the presence of God in their lives.

The psalms began to be written during the **Diaspora,** a time when the Hebrew people were broken up and scattered. This time of history helped to shape a tremendously powerful and beautiful spirituality among the Hebrew people. They longed for a homeland and a sacred place since the Temple had been destroyed. In the midst of this struggle, the Hebrew people discovered a profound dependence on and intimacy with God.

. . . . The Prayer of Assembly . . . .

The psalms grow out of this struggle, this desire to rely on the love and promise that God had made to his people. They reflect the spiritual journey of the Hebrew people in a way nothing else does.

The psalms are powerful prayers for us today. Praying them expresses the struggles and joys of our own spiritual journey. They challenge us to root our lives in our faith. Coming to know and respond to God in love is what we were created to do. Our identity is in God, who made us in his image.

The psalms can be hymns of praise and thanks, prayers, cries of hope or lamentations. They still express the simplicity and the spontaneity of prayer. We pray from our hearts what we experience in our lives. Whether flowing from joy or pain, frustration or anger, hope or anxiousness, fear or desire, the psalms express our trust in God, who accepts us in our good times and our bad times.

We believe that God created us out of love and continues to reach out to us in that love. In prayer we bring to God who we are—with no disguise or falseness. If we are sad, angry, happy, or joyous; if we are anxious and preoccupied with other things in our life, that is the time when God accepts and embraces us.

A careful praying of the psalms is at the heart of our prayer as Christians as it is for Jews. Our struggle to come to know God through our prayer life grows out of the same soil as our ancestors.

Moses, statue by Michelangelo (1475–1564).

Prayer

❖ ❖ ❖

God of wonder and grace,

enter into my heart and help me

to see your face.

My ancestors carved a path

for me to know you;

help me find the wisdom

in their journey.

Give me the desire

to know you more fully.

I am your child,

and you are my God.

Grant that I might become

the person that you created.

Help me to realize the wonder

that you created in me,

and teach me to love you

in all that I do.

Amen.

REVIEW

IMPORTANT TERMS TO KNOW

Covenant of Sinai—the Covenant between God and the people of Israel. By the Covenant of Sinai the Israelites became the special people of Yahweh (see Exodus 19).

Diaspora—the Jewish communities that settled outside Palestine that began in the eighth century B.C.

Hebrews—the name given to the Israelites by non-Israelites

hesed—a Hebrew word attributed to God, meaning "all merciful, loving, and unconditional"

People of God—a term used to signify the people of the covenant

prophet—a person sent by God to clearly speak out and call people back to living their covenant relationship with God and one another

Revelation—God making himself known to us

Sacred Tradition—the living transmission accomplished in the Holy Spirit, by the Church. "[T]he Church, in her doctrine, life, and worship perpetuates and transmits to every generation all that she herself is, all that she believes" (CCC, 78).

CHAPTER SUMMARY

The Old Testament story of God's people is the story of a people of prayer. In this chapter we learned:

1. God invites each person to a mysterious encounter with himself. This encounter is known as prayer.

2. Prayer unfolds throughout the whole history of salvation as a reciprocal call between God and man.

3. The prayer of Abraham is a prayer of faith. The prayer of Moses is an example of the prayer of intercession.

4. The prayer of the People of God flourished during the time of the kings and prophets. King David prays for his people and in their name. The prayer of the prophet Elijah is the prayer of conversion, calling the People of God back to the love of God.

5. The psalms are the masterwork of prayer in the Old Testament. They are also an essential dimension of Christian prayer.

EXPLORING OUR CATHOLIC FAITH

1. Listening to God's Word

Prayerfully read Psalm 118 (a praise psalm), Psalm 107 (a psalm of thanksgiving), Psalm 3, 4, or 5 (a psalm of lament), and Psalm 11, 16, or 23 (a psalm of trust). Reflect on your own needs and desires of God at this moment of your life. Then compose your own psalm in your journal.

2. Understanding the Teachings of the Catholic Church

The *Catechism* teaches, "In prayer, the faithful God's initiative of love always comes first; our own first step is always a response" (CCC, 2567). Discuss the meaning and implications of this teaching.

3. Reflecting on Our Catholic Faith

Saint Ambrose shares this insight about the psalms with us: "Yes, a psalm is a blessing on the lips of the people, praise of God, the assembly's homage, a general acclamation, a word that speaks for all, the voice of the Church, a confession of faith in song." What is the meaning of these thoughts for your life? Write your thoughts in your journal.

4. Living Our Catholic Faith

The prayer of Moses is an example of intercessory prayer. His prayer flowed from his trust in the faithfulness of God and his understanding of and compassion for his people. What are the needs and struggles of the people you know or know about? Write and pray a prayer of intercession, trusting in God's faithfulness.

CHAPTER 3

In the Fullness of Time

"Blessed be the Lord, the God of Israel,
for he has visited and brought redemption
to his people."

LUKE 1:68

Answer the following questions:

What have you learned about prayer from other people?

How do you use imagination in prayer?

One of the greatest films of all times is *The Ten Commandments*. Cecil B. de Mille set new standards for spectacular crowd scenes and special effects. In one of the most dramatic and memorable scenes, Moses goes up the mountain and receives the Ten Commandments amid thunder and lightning. Then, his face changes in appearance and Moses returns to his people. His whole countenance glows a brilliant white—a sign that he has come face-to-face with God.

KEY TERMS

conversion

solitude

Many people have experiences of God—although they probably are not nearly as dramatic as what Moses experienced. Describe an experience of God you have had.

Road toward Saint Catherine Monastery, Sinai, Egypt.

The Ten Commandments have been revealed to us by God. They help us know God's will and live as the People of God. Jesus is the fulfillment of God's Revelation. He is "the way and the truth and the life" (John 14:6). By patience and taking time to reflect on the life of Jesus and on the Tradition of our Church, we are better able to understand the importance of prayer on our journey with God. By listening to the Word of God, by reading about the insights of our ancestors in faith, by participating in the sacred liturgy—especially the Eucharist—we can deepen our understanding of the presence of God in our lives.

In the last chapter we focused on God as he has revealed himself in the Old Testament. The prayerful struggle of the Israelites to know and love God reflects our own desire to be connected heart-to-heart with God as well. In this chapter we will reflect on the life, message, and example of Jesus, who provides for us most fully a picture of God-in-the-fullness of time.

(*Catechism of the Catholic Church*, 2598–2606)

God Is Revealed in Christ

The Israelites came to know God as one who was deeply intimate with them. Prayer for them became a *conversation* between the people and their Creator. We too are invited to become intimate with our God through Jesus. The Spirit calls us to listen to God's voice, wherever that voice comes from, and to be open to God's presence at every moment of every day. We are invited to spend time with Jesus and hear how he teaches us to pray.

Prayer requires listening. Listening requires patience. Patience is a discipline just as prayer is a discipline. It is through the experience of our inner selves, our inner life, that we are able to meet God. It is through moments of prayer that we are able to enter into a more intimate relationship with our Creator.

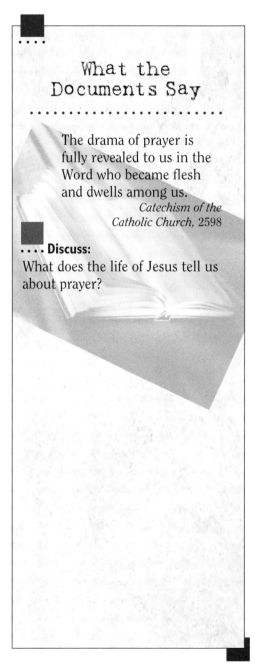

What the Documents Say

The drama of prayer is fully revealed to us in the Word who became flesh and dwells among us.
Catechism of the Catholic Church, 2598

Discuss:
What does the life of Jesus tell us about prayer?

Jesus Prays

As Jesus learned the prayerful rhythms of his tradition, we too look to our own Christian traditions to help us probe deeper into our own spirituality. Jesus' prayer is rooted in that deeper source. He hints at that source when he affirms the need to "be in my Father's house" (Luke 2:49).

Central to our Christian faith is the belief that the Son of God became flesh in Jesus for the Salvation and Redemption of the human race and to make it once again "whole." In their book *Pray with All Your Senses,* Lo-Ann and David Trembley (ACTA Publications, 1997) write that "We human beings are not whole. We live in broken little pieces. Although God created us for joy and freedom, we live stuck in ruts and trapped in worn-out patterns."

. . . ."Abba, Father". . . . . . .

Jesus gives us a glimpse of our relationship with God as Father, or as "Abba." Jesus teaches us that prayer is love-centered, a trust-centered conversation.

Who is God? Who am I? What does it mean to be a creature made in the image and likeness of God? How can I know God? Are my prayers groundless, going into thin air, into nothingness? Or do they find a home in the heart of God? These are questions that we often ask in the midst of our groping for truth and certainty. It is through the window of Jesus that we are able to see God most clearly. If we want to know who God is and what God wants of us, we look to Jesus.

For Reflection

Our imagination is a powerful tool for us. It is one of the many windows through which God manifests himself to us. Describe how you use your imagination when you pray.

The Spirit Guides Us

As we engage in our own spiritual journeys, we are reminded that we are not making that trek alone. No person is sufficient unto themselves. We are created as social beings who find meaning in our interconnectedness with others, with the world around us, and, most importantly, with God.

Jesus did not engage in his ministry alone. He conversed in prayer with his Father. The Spirit accompanied him (Luke 4:18).

We find Jesus joining with the Spirit at every turn, every juncture, every decision, before all the major events of his life. He brought with him the profound direction of the Spirit of God.

Jesus sought out and found direction from sources outside himself—sources that were true to his mission. He sought out the wisdom of his ancestors while in the Temple among the elders. We too need to be attentive to the voice of the Spirit, the voice of wisdom within our tradition.

Jesus Models Prayer

Jesus taught his prayer to his followers by the way he prayed. Through this thoughtful and contemplative posture, the disciples came to learn how to pray from the master of prayer. They came to know the love of and way to God. His followers believed that, and we, his followers today, believe that too. As the disciples learned from Jesus the way to pray, so too do we look to Jesus as the model for our Christian prayer.

. . . . . Prayer of Solitude . . . . .

Today we hear much about "centering" prayer. Groups are formed to help people find a focus to their lives. People are joining self-help groups in record numbers, attempting to find direction and purpose to their lives. Retreat centers around the country are seeing more people than ever who not only are seeking spiritual direction but are responding to a deep hunger for a quiet place to listen to the voice of God.

Two thousand years ago Jesus modeled this kind of prayer to his disciples. In doing so Jesus taught his followers that there is an art to "centering" their lives on God.

We might feel that we would be wasting time by not *doing* something and simply "take the time" to be alone, focused on God. By doing so we become engaged in the sacred moments of life in a way unlike any other. We are able to present ourselves to God in an unencumbered manner. Our prayer then becomes "Here I am" (1 Samuel 3:16).

Jesus often went away in **solitude** to be alone, to meet God. Time alone enabled Jesus to focus and center on what God was calling him to do. To be able to come to a quiet place in the interior of our heart is an indispensable tool necessary for our genuine spiritual growth.

When we come to God in prayer, we often do all the talking. For many of us prayer becomes a one-way street. It comes from us, to God. We do not allow time for our listening to God, who is present in our hearts and souls. We are so busy "doing" things that we fail to recognize the presence of God in our daily lives.

In modeling the prayer of solitude, Jesus models an uncluttered place for us to pray—a place for us just to *be* with God. This is where we are called— to the solitude of our hearts and souls,

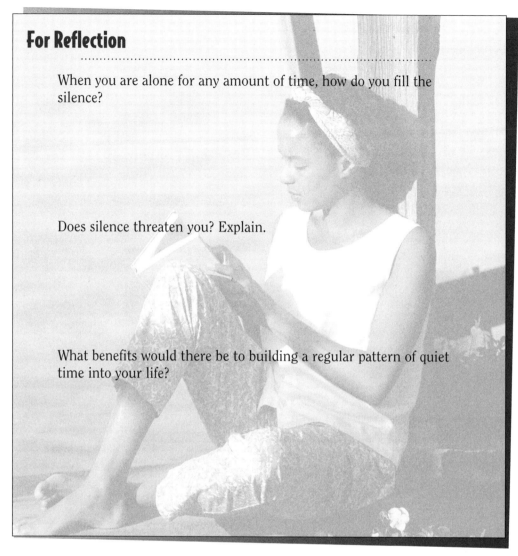

For Reflection

When you are alone for any amount of time, how do you fill the silence?

Does silence threaten you? Explain.

What benefits would there be to building a regular pattern of quiet time into your life?

to a life that is lived from the interior, from the inside *out*.

In his prayer of solitude, Jesus, who is both fully man and fully God, reveals something extraordinary about our identity as human beings. We are invited to share in the sacredness of life. Jesus shares our humanity and affirms our ultimate goodness in the eyes of God. The prayer of Jesus is rooted in the depths of his soul. Planted in the midst of his humanness, his prayer flows from the same struggle each of us faces in our journey to God. "The whole prayer of Jesus is contained in this loving adherence of his human heart to the mystery of the will of the Father" (CCC, 2603).

. . . . Prayer of Thanksgiving . . . .

As we look to Jesus as a model for our prayer, we discover in him a heart that is grateful to God. It is an attitude at the heart of who he is. Jesus is aware of the constant presence of God in all of creation, in the hearts and souls of human beings. As we pray on our own journey, we are invited to imitate Jesus in his manner of prayer.

Welling up from the depths of his soul, originating in the heart of God, the prayer of Jesus embraces all of humanity. Jesus teaches us that in prayer we too are caught up in the interconnectedness of all human beings. Genuine Christian prayer both connects us to God and fuses us to others. We are the Body of Christ. Christian prayer celebrates and affirms our responsibility to and connection with the community of believers and with all others.

Reflecting on the ways that Jesus prayed and modeling our own prayer on Jesus' prayer, we are able to discover our own relationship with God.

(CCC, 2607–2616)

Jesus Teaches Us How to Pray

Key to the prayer of Jesus, and that which is essential if we are to learn anything from him as our teacher, is the fact that Jesus prays from *who he is*. Jesus' prayer reveals his relationship with his Father and the Spirit. To be a Christian is more than adhering to a set of beliefs about God; it is a living *relationship* with God in Christ with the Holy Spirit.

As a Jew, Jesus teaches us about the roots of our faith in the history of the Israelites and the Covenant that God invited them to enter into with him. He reveals to us the newness of the coming of the Kingdom of God through the parables. Finally Jesus shares his relationship with God with us so that we too might engage others in a journey of faith.

Prayer of Conversion

The message of Jesus was one of **conversion,** or in Greek, a word meaning *metanoia.* "From the *Sermon on the Mount* onwards, Jesus insists on *conversion of heart.* . . . This filial conversion is entirely directed to the Father" (CCC, 2608). For Jesus, this meant a changing, or turn around, of the direction of one's life, a discarding of the old ways of acting, being, and behaving, and centering one's life on God.

Jesus' call to conversion challenges us to forgive others when we are harmed. We are to love our enemies and pray for those who persecute us. We are to pray to God in "secret" and not be "showy" about our faith. We are to seek God above everything else.

We are often invited to chase our material dreams with the promise that "finite goods" will satisfy our heart's desire for meaning. It is a difficult task to live a faith-centered life when our life is turned in this direction. Faith, first, seeks God. It is life-moving, life-changing. Faith is believing and trusting God. When this becomes the focus of our life, we are turned in a different direction. We become someone new and different from before. We truly begin to love God with all our hearts, our minds, our strength, and our souls, and to love our neighbors as ourselves.

For Reflection

What kinds of things do you "hold on to" that keep you from centering your life on God?

How does your relationship with God have an impact on your life?

.... Discuss:

To have a genuine spirituality, one must move first in the direction of God—seek first the Kingdom of God.

Prayer in Jesus' Name

Jesus teaches us that our prayers, when united with his, draw us closer to God. We are taught that God grants us what we ask for. "[A]ll that you ask for in prayer, believe that you will receive it and it shall be yours" (Mark 11:24). We are promised that if we pray in Jesus' name, God will provide for us. "Until now you have not asked anything in my name; ask and you will receive, so that your joy may be complete" (John 16:24).

Jesus not only teaches us to pray to the Father, he also tells us "ask in my name" (John 14:13) and assures us that our prayer will be heard when it is united with his. "In the Holy Spirit, Christian prayer is a communion of love with the Father, not only through Christ but also *in him*" (CCC, 2615).

Jesus teaches us that God answers prayers and our effort does not go unnoticed. However, what we pray for may not always be granted exactly according to our expectations and timetable. But we do believe God *always* responds in our best interests. God writes the answers to our prayers within the patterns and rhythms of our lives. We often miss the responding voice of God because we have become too wrapped up in our lives to notice the ordinary ways that he answers us.

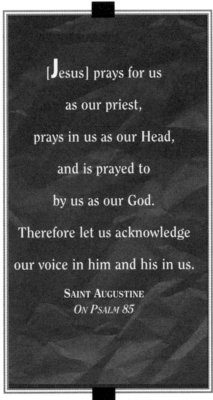

[Jesus] prays for us as our priest, prays in us as our Head, and is prayed to by us as our God. Therefore let us acknowledge our voice in him and his in us.

SAINT AUGUSTINE
ON PSALM 85

(CCC, 2617–2619)

The Prayer of Mary

Mary is a model of prayer for Christians. Her prayers "are characterized by the generous offering of her whole being in faith" (CCC, 2622).

At the Annunciation when she is chosen to be the mother of God's Son, she responds in faith. She cooperates in a unique way with the Father's plan of loving-kindness for our Salvation. "Behold, I am the handmaid of the Lord," she responds. "May it be done to me according to your word" (Luke 1:38).

At the wedding feast at Cana, in trust she orders the servers, "Do whatever he tells you" (John 2:5). At Pentecost she is gathered in prayer with the disciples, awaiting the fulfillment of Jesus' promise to send the Spirit. (See Acts 1:14.)

Prayerfully read these Gospel passages, which describe Jesus and prayer. Write down a brief description of what you learn about prayer from each passage.

Matthew 14:22–23   Luke 6:12–13

Luke 5:15–16   Mark 1:35

· · · · Discuss:

How do these passages help you understand the role of prayer in your life?

Prayer

❖ ❖ ❖

My soul proclaims the greatness
of the Lord,
my spirit rejoices in God
my Savior;
for he has looked with favor on
his lowly servant.
From this day all
generations will call me blessed:
the Almighty has done
great things for me,
and holy is his Name.
He has mercy on those who
fear him
in every generation.
He has shown the strength
of his arm,
he has scattered the proud in
their conceit.
He has cast down the
mighty from their thrones,
and has lifted up the lowly.
He has filled the hungry with
good things,
and the rich he has sent
away empty.
He has come to the help of his
servant Israel
for he has remembered his
promise of mercy,
the promise he made to our
fathers,
to Abraham and his
children forever.

Catholic Household Blessings and Prayers
See Luke 1:46–55 (Magnificat)

REVIEW

IMPORTANT TERMS TO KNOW

conversion—a change in which a person adopts a new way of thinking, or a deeper religious commitment

solitude—the experience of being alone, without the distractions and the noise of our world

CHAPTER SUMMARY

True prayer is fully revealed to us in Jesus, the Word of God who became flesh and lived among us. In this chapter we learned:

1. The prayer of Jesus is the perfect model of prayer.

2. Jesus' prayer is marked by conversion of heart, faith, and filial boldness.

3. Jesus invites us to pray in his name. Jesus assures us that our prayers are heard.

4. Christian prayer brings us in union with the love of the Father. In the Holy Spirit, we are united to the Father not only through Christ but also in him.

5. Mary is a model of prayer. Her whole life was marked by faith. The prayers of Mary demonstrate the total giving of her life in faith to God.

EXPLORING OUR CATHOLIC FAITH

1. Listening to God's Word

The Gospel of Luke contains three principal parables on prayer. They are Luke 11:5–13, Luke 18:1–8, and Luke 18:9–14. Prayerfully read and reflect on one of these parables. What is Luke teaching about prayer? List the important points and discuss your ideas.

2. Understanding the Teachings of the Catholic Church

Through the prayers of the Church we profess and celebrate our faith. We conclude the Eucharistic Prayer by saying or singing the Doxology: "Through him, with him, in him, in the unity of the Holy Spirit, all glory and honor is yours, almighty Father, for ever and ever. Amen." How does this Doxology manifest the nature of Christian prayer?

3. Reflecting on Our Catholic Faith

Jesus is our model of prayer. The Gospels are filled with examples of Jesus in prayer. Write a reflection in your journal on the prayer life of Jesus.

4. Living Our Catholic Faith

Spend some time praying in solitude.

CHAPTER 4

The Church, a Living History of Gratitude

When the time for Pentecost was fulfilled,
they were all in one place together. . . .
And they were all filled with the holy Spirit
and began to speak in different tongues,
as the Spirit enabled them to proclaim.

ACTS 2:1, 4

We are all rooted in our histories. We cannot divorce ourselves from our past. We learn from the failures as well as from the victories of our past. If we fall and hit our head, resulting in a loss of memory, we say that we have a case of amnesia. We have no memory of our past.

If we forget our past, the meaning of our present lives, and consequently, our future, is diminished. Imagine the difficulty of attempting to build a vision for the future if we have forgotten who we were and where we came from.

KEY TERMS

prayer of adoration and blessing

prayer of intercession

prayer of petition

prayer of praise

prayer of thanksgiving

What are the happiest moments of your past?

What are some things from your past that are helping to build your future?

[41]

Our tradition of prayer as Catholics has a past. Its memory is kept alive by the Spirit of God dwelling with us. "The Advocate," Jesus promised, "the holy Spirit that the Father will send in my name—he will teach you everything and remind you of all that [I] told you" (John 14:26). Recognizing the wisdom that emerges from our past, beginning with the Old Testament, is an indispensable piece of the puzzle of our Christian prayer life.

Often people dismiss the wisdom that is born out of the experience of our ancestors as "old" and, therefore, meaningless. In this chapter we will explore the struggle and the questions that drove the early Christian community to grasp and cling to the person and message of Jesus. It is here that we can begin to identify with the first Christians in our search for a more meaningful prayer experience.

(Catechism of the Catholic Church, 2623–2625)

The Prayer of the Church

At the Last Supper Jesus charged the disciples to keep his memory alive. Paul writes:

> For I received from the Lord what I also handed on to you, that the Lord Jesus, on the night he was handed over, took bread, and after he had given thanks, broke it and said, "This is my body that is for you. Do this in remembrance of me." In the same way also the cup, after supper, saying, "This cup is the new covenant in my blood. Do this, as often as you drink it, in remembrance of me."
>
> **I Corinthians 11:23–25**

It was in the convening days after the Death and Resurrection of Jesus, in the midst of their confusion, born of loss and grief, that the disciples would begin to shape and form their prayer—in remembrance of Jesus. They struggled to unravel their profound experience of God in Jesus. No longer was their Teacher present in the same way as before. Their relationship with Jesus had had a life-changing effect on them. His Resurrection had presented them with a new way of thinking, had challenged their understanding of life itself. As a result they began to build a life upon their faith in the risen Lord. It was in and through their own prayers and devotions that their future was given form and definition.

In the Book of the Acts of the Apostles, we are told that the disciples devoted themselves to prayer. It was the Spirit who taught and formed the Church in the life of prayer. It was in this experience that they found their mission and were able to clarify their Christian vision. Having a solid background in the tradition of their Jewish prayer, especially in their praying of the Scriptures, the followers of Jesus began to build a characteristically unique style of prayer that would reflect their faith in Christ.

Central to our Catholic spirituality is the experience of the presence of Christ in the Eucharist. The words "This bread is my body. . . . This cup is the cup of my blood," would echo and vibrate into the marrow of their bones. It was imperative to keep the memory of Jesus alive and his mission prospering.

The prayer of the Apostles and the first Christian communities would give shape to and would form a unique

Read and reflect on this passage from the Acts of the Apostles.

> They devoted themselves to the teaching of the apostles and to the communal life, to the breaking of the bread and to the prayers. . . . Every day they devoted themselves to meeting together in the temple area and to breaking bread in their homes. They ate their meals with exultation and sincerity of heart, praising God and enjoying favor with all the people.
>
> Acts 2:42, 46–47

. . . . Discuss:

How did the early Christians devote themselves to the teachings of the Apostles? List ways you can "devote yourself to prayer." Choose one and explain how you could make it a part of your life.

spirituality, a following of "the way." The prayer of the Church would quickly and clearly be characterized by three things: founded on the apostolic faith, authenticated by charity, and nourished in the Eucharist.

At Pentecost the Holy Spirit filled the disciples gathered in the upper room. We are told that the disciples were so overwhelmed with the Spirit that they began to speak in languages other than their own, and that those who heard them speak, each heard them speak in their own language. From this point onward, their lives would be reshaped. Their practice of prayer would continue to be crafted using their Jewish tradition. New forms, born out of their faith in Christ, would evolve that would nourish the spirituality of Christians to the present time.

(CCC, 2626–2643)

Forms of Prayer

God loves us. The heart of our faith is this simple truth. The peoples of the Old Testament knew and believed this. Mary and Joseph believed this. John the Baptist was driven by his love of God to call people to repent and be saved. The Incarnation of the Son of God is an act of divine love. "For God so loved the world that he gave his only Son, so that everyone who believes in him might . . . have eternal life" (John 3:16). This love is a gift. Once accepted, we are never the same.

Blessing and Adoration

God is the source of every blessing. Life, love, everything that is good is ultimately a gift because God, out of love, chose to create and to save. In response to God's "blessing" us, we in turn "bless" God.

Our life is filled with the love of God. Through this love of God we come to the truth of our own lives. True happiness is found here. God's love is the origin and end of our happiness.

Prayer of Blessing. The **prayer of blessing** expresses the basic movement of Christian prayer. It is an encounter between human beings and God. The prayer of blessing is our response to God, who out of unconditional love blesses us. The human heart in return blesses God, who is the source of all blessing.

Our prayer is lifted up to heaven and through the grace of the Holy Spirit the love of God moves through Christ and blesses us.

Blessed be the God and Father of our Lord Jesus Christ, who has blessed us in Christ with every spiritual blessing in the heavens. . . . In him you also, who have heard the word of truth, the gospel of your salvation, and have believed in him, were sealed with the promised holy Spirit, which is the first installment of our inheritance toward redemption as God's possession, to the praise of his glory.

Ephesians 1:3, 13–14

God's Blessing in My Life

Quietly reflect on your life—past, present, and hoped-for future. List your blessings.

Pray:
Bless God for blessing you!

Prayer of Adoration. The **prayer of adoration** exalts the greatness of God who made us.

Enter, let us bow down in worship;
let us kneel before the LORD who made us.

For this is our God,
whose people we are,
God's well-tended flock.

Psalm 95:6–7

Adoring some*thing* is different from adoring God. The word *adore* suggests a particular "posture," both intellectual and emotional. The posture of adoration calls for a humble heart. Humility is an extraordinary gift. A heart that is humble, made of flesh and pliable, is prepared to meet God. A humble heart allows us to be open to God and enter his presence with us in our life. The prayer of adoration is a gift of the Spirit that fills us with "the spirit of awe and wonder" in the presence of God.

Petition

If we look up the word *pray* in the thesaurus, we would find words like *beg, plead, implore, entreat, conjure, beseech,* and *desire.* It is interesting that the act of praying is so often linked only to the act of "asking" for something. While prayer is more than asking for something, it is clear that our needs are to be expressed in prayer. Wisdom, however, in knowing what to ask for is the heart of our **prayer of petition.**

What the Roman Missal Says

During Mass at the beginning of the Liturgy of the Eucharist we pray:
    Blessed are you,
        Lord God of all creation,
    for through your goodness
        we have received
    the bread we offer you:
    fruit of the earth
        and work of human hands,
    it will become for us the
        bread of life.

Roman Missal

Discuss some specific gifts of creation that you can include in your prayers.

Read and reflect on this teaching about prayer passed on to us in the Letter to the Romans.

In the same way, the Spirit too comes to the aid of our weakness; for we do not know how to pray as we ought, but the Spirit itself intercedes with inexpressible groanings.

ROMANS 8:26

···· Discuss:

Jesus promised us that the Spirit is our Advocate. In what ways does Romans 8:26 help you understand the meaning of Christian prayer?

The prayer of petition is a prayer form that expresses our dependence on God and our faith and trust that he cares for us.

> "So do not worry and say, 'What are we to eat?' or 'What are we to drink?' or 'What are we to wear?' All these things the pagans seek. Your heavenly Father knows that you need them all. But seek first the kingdom [of God] and his righteousness, and all these things will be given you besides."
> **Matthew 6:31–33**

The prayer of petition is also called supplication. This is a prayer that God will supply for our needs. The *Catechism* teaches us that there are three movements to the prayer of petition, or supplication. They are: asking for forgiveness, every need, and the desire and search for the kingdom to come.

Asking for Forgiveness. Human beings sin. We tend to act selfishly. We turn away from God. We don't always seek what is necessarily good for us or for others around us. Sometimes, maybe more often than not, we give in to temptations that are self-destructive and leave us alone and lonely. Our petition is our turning back to God.

Because we sin, the first step or "movement" of the prayer of petition is asking forgiveness. Of course one must have a humble heart for this movement to be genuine. "O God, be merciful to me a sinner" was the plea of the tax collector (Luke 18:13). The necessity

for forgiveness, and the humility that leads us to that realization, is unavoidable if our prayer is to be pure and authentic. Jesus tells us that we "receive from him whatever we ask" (1 John 3:22). It is the asking and the receiving of forgiveness that makes way for both Eucharistic and personal prayer. Forgiveness removes what stands between ourselves and God.

Every Need. In the Old Testament we find a prayer form used in times of trouble and need. Sometimes called the prayer of lamentation, it expresses the groaning hearts of the People of God, waiting for him to save them from their distress.

Through the psalms we come to know that our experiences of frustration and struggle are echoed in the prayers of the Israelites. One of the characteristics of the prayer of the Israelites was that they brought *who they were* to their prayer. They openly and straightforwardly placed their needs and feelings before God. In the Old Testament we can read not only their joys but their distress as well.

The New Testament adds a unique dimension of hope to the prayer of Christians. Here we find, in the wake of the risen Christ, a unique sense of hope flowing from the early Christian belief in the imminent return of Jesus to redeem all of creation.

Kingdom of God. Jesus taught his disciples to pray,

> Our Father in heaven,
>   hallowed be your name,
>   your kingdom come,
>   your will be done,
>   on earth as in heaven.

Before all else the Christian prayer of petition seeks the coming of the kingdom. The establishment and fulfillment of the kingdom is the plan of the Father and the mission and work of Christ and the Holy Spirit.

Intercession

If ever we were to pray as Jesus did, it is here, in the intercessory prayers. "He is the one intercessor with the Father on behalf of all men, especially sinners" (CCC, 2634; see Romans 8:34; 1 John 2:1; 1 Timothy 2:5–8). Since Abraham, the **prayer of intercession**—asking on the behalf of another—"has been characteristic of a heart attuned to God's mercy" (CCC, 2635).

Christian prayer of intercession knows no boundaries. It moves us out of ourselves to address the needs of others—whether we know them, are comfortable with them, or even if they have harmed us.

Because God is love, we inherit the task to love, to bring order out of chaos, to be Christ in the world. In intercessory prayer we lift the needs of all people to the heart of God through Jesus Christ. We respond to God's call to tend to the hearts of others. The needs of our brothers and sisters are our own needs.

Recently research was done to find out whether intercessory prayer made any significant difference in people's lives. A group of people were gathered to pray for the needs of another group whose members were suffering from various illnesses. It was discovered that many in the latter group experienced a positive effect in their overall health as a result of the prayers said on their behalf.

We are the Body of Christ. As Saint Paul tells us, just as one part of the body is affected, so is the whole body affected. In praying for others, we are in turn praying for ourselves as we all are connected in the Spirit of God.

Journal Writing:

When was the last time you prayed for someone?

When do you pray for others? How often?

What are your hopes and expectations when you pray for others?

Thanksgiving

Life is a glorious mystery. Our existence is a gift. When we finally discover these truths and believe them, our spontaneous response is gratitude and thanksgiving to God.

Christians are people of thanksgiving. The Eucharist is the central prayer of the Christian community. It is the great **prayer of thanksgiving** of the Church.

> The Eucharist is a sacrifice of thanksgiving to the Father, a blessing by which the Church expresses her gratitude to God for all his benefits, for all that he has accomplished through creation, redemption, and sanctification. Eucharist means first of all "thanksgiving." CCC, 1360

Paul so often mirrored this basic attitude of the followers of Christ in his writings. "In all circumstances give thanks," he wrote, "for this is the will of God for you in Christ Jesus" (1 Thessalonians 5:18).

Being grateful is synonymous with being Christian. We realize that all that we have is a gift and that God is the Giver. We are completely reliant on God for all we have.

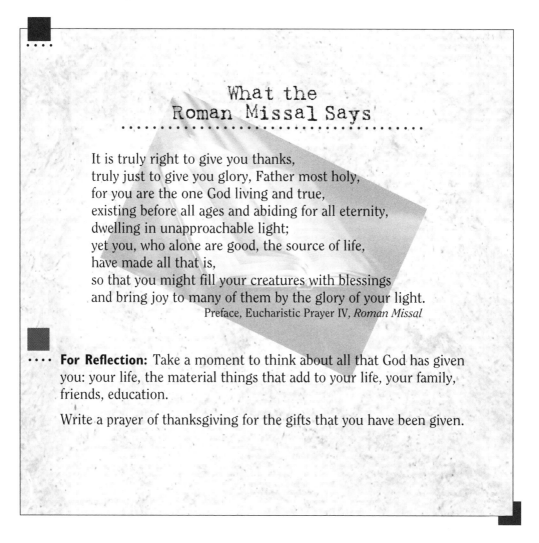

What the Roman Missal Says

It is truly right to give you thanks,
truly just to give you glory, Father most holy,
for you are the one God living and true,
existing before all ages and abiding for all eternity,
dwelling in unapproachable light;
yet you, who alone are good, the source of life,
have made all that is,
so that you might fill your creatures with blessings
and bring joy to many of them by the glory of your light.

Preface, Eucharistic Prayer IV, *Roman Missal*

For Reflection: Take a moment to think about all that God has given you: your life, the material things that add to your life, your family, friends, education.

Write a prayer of thanksgiving for the gifts that you have been given.

Praise

In the 70s Merlin Carothers wrote two books entitled *The Power of Praise* and *Praise the Lord Anyway!* Carothers suggested that the **prayer of praise** was powerful because in praising God we enter into a level of intimacy with God that cannot be duplicated. In the prayer of praise we give praise to God for *everything* in our life, the good *and* the bad. We acknowledge that bad and good which are part of our life lead us to God. It is our faith and trust in God that lead us to see that everything in our life is in some way connected to God. In our prayer of praise, we applaud God's love for us and caring presence with us in good times and bad. The prayer of praise is our recognition of God's ever faithful, caring presence in our lives. We express our faith that God is the "I am who am" (Exodus 3:14). We become Moses, taking off our shoes because we are on holy ground, face-to-face with the Almighty Creator and Lover of our being. Prayers of praise give glory to God, beyond the great deeds he has done, but simply because HE IS.

Journal Writing:

Take twenty minutes and reflect on your life.

List all those elements of your life for which you can give God praise.

Prayer

❖ ❖ ❖

Hear, O Israel!

The Lord is our God,
the Lord alone!

Blessed is God's glorious
kingdom for ever and
ever.

You shall love the Lord,
your God,
with all your mind,

and with all your soul,
and with all your strength.

Amen.

SH'M A ISRAEL

IMPORTANT TERMS TO KNOW

prayer of adoration and blessing— prayer that declares God as our Creator and the source of all blessings

prayer of intercession—prayer that prays for all people, even those who have harmed us

prayer of petition—prayer that expresses our faith and trust in God

prayer of praise—prayer that praises God for everything in our life, both the good and the bad

prayer of thanksgiving—prayer that expresses our gratitude to God for all his blessings

CHAPTER SUMMARY

The Church has a rich history of prayer. These prayers developed into a wealth of prayer forms. In this chapter we learned:

1. The prayer of Christians has its roots in the ancient prayers of the Hebrew people.

2. Out of the experience of the disciples of Jesus came a unique Christian prayer that combined the richness of the Hebrew tradition and the Spirit of Jesus.

3. The human heart returns blessings to God, the source of all blessings, because God blesses us.

4. All of our needs are objects of prayers of petition.

5. Prayers of intercession know no boundaries and consist in asking on behalf of another and even our enemies.

6. Everything in our life, joys and sufferings, can be a prayer of thanksgiving.

7. Prayers of praise rise to God not only for what he has done, but simply because HE IS.

EXPLORING OUR CATHOLIC FAITH

1. Listening to God's Word

Jesus taught us to pray always—and he never grew tired of prayer. Read the parable that Jesus used to make this point: Luke 18:1–8. Discuss how your prayer will be persistent.

2. Understanding the Teachings of the Catholic Church

The discovery of intimacy with God, the necessity for adoration, the need for intercession—the experience of Christian holiness shows us the fruitfulness of prayer, in which God reveals himself to the spirit and heart of his servants (*Apostolic Exhortation on the Renewal of Religious Life,* 43). In what ways do the forms of prayer affect your relationship with God?

3. Reflecting on Our Catholic Faith

The five prayer forms discussed in this chapter have been used for hundreds of years in the Catholic Church. Discuss examples of how you have used these prayers or experienced these prayers in the Catholic Church.

4. Living Our Catholic Faith

Spend some time in prayer, using at least two of the different prayer forms.

CHAPTER 5

Living Water

"Whoever believes in me, as scripture says:
'Rivers of living water will flow from
within him.'"

JOHN 7:38

What Do You Think?

Complete the following sentences:

Some sources of prayer are . . .

Prayer can be addressed to . . .

When I pray, I usually pray to . . .

The people who teach us to pray are . . .

A woman of Samaria came to draw water.

Jesus said to her, "Give me a drink."

His disciples had gone into the town to buy food.

The Samaritan woman said to him, "How can you, a Jew, ask me, a Samaritan woman, for a drink?" (For Jews use nothing in common with Samaritans.)

Jesus answered and said to her, "If you knew the gift of God, and who is saying to you, 'Give me a drink,' you would have asked him, and he would have given you living water."

The woman said to him, "Sir, give me this water, so that I may never be thirsty or have to keep coming here to draw water."

Based on John 4:7–16

What are some things for which you thirst? How do you quench that thirst? What can Jesus do to satisfy your thirst?

The Woman of Samaria by Danish artist Carl Heinrich Bloch (1834–1890).

KEY TERMS

charity

faith

hope

liturgy

Theological Virtues

As the Samaritan woman did, we too come to Jesus to be nourished. We recognize our need for God. We face our thirst and ask that it be quenched. Jesus promises that the thirst of those who believe will be satisfied. In our hunger and thirst, we lay our needs before God. We are called and invited to the wellsprings, to the places of healing and nourishment. In this chapter we will explore more deeply our Catholic tradition of prayer.

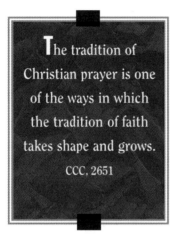

The tradition of Christian prayer is one of the ways in which the tradition of faith takes shape and grows.

CCC, 2651

(Catechism of the Catholic Church, 2650–2652)

Fed by the Holy Spirit

We are made in the image and likeness of God. We have been created to seek the love and presence of God. This means that we have an innate desire to know and love God.

The Spirit Is Our Teacher

Given our spiritual hunger, it is important to discover places in our lives where we can go to be fed, to be nourished. The Holy Spirit leads us to those places in our lives. We need to learn to listen and acquire ears of faith. Truly it is the Holy Spirit that teaches us how to pray. If we are ignorant of the sources of spiritual direction and nourishment, then our faith weakens and our spiritual roots wither and may even fade away.

If our faith is to grow, we need to take the necessary time to pray, and to pray well. In order to pray well, we must have the will to pray and take the time to learn how to pray. We must open our mind and heart to the one who teaches us to pray, the Spirit dwelling within us.

The Practice of Prayer

If we are to be good at doing anything, we must develop the habits, skills, and discipline necessary to be successful. Just as there are very few "natural" athletes, there are very few people who find it *easy* to pray. It takes practice, practice, practice. Basketball and volleyball players might spend several hours a day, day after day, just practicing.

Practice, practice, practice. This is how they will improve their skills and broaden their understanding of the game. They will listen to their coaches and watch and learn from other people who are better and more skilled. They will seek the advice of mentors and combine all the wisdom and experience of these role models to create a style of play that is uniquely theirs.

We learn from the experience and wisdom of others. We do not live in a vacuum—unaffected by the ideas and actions of other people. It is important to know that the Holy Spirit works

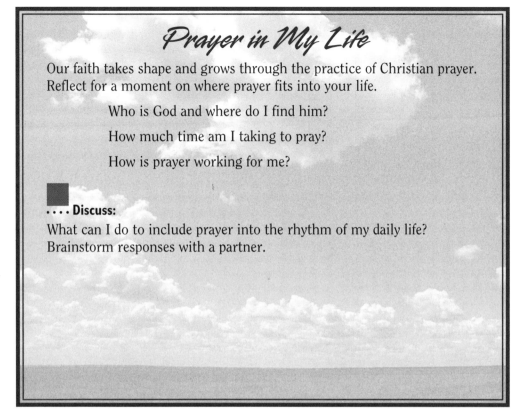

Prayer in My Life

Our faith takes shape and grows through the practice of Christian prayer. Reflect for a moment on where prayer fits into your life.

Who is God and where do I find him?

How much time am I taking to pray?

How is prayer working for me?

.... Discuss:

What can I do to include prayer into the rhythm of my daily life? Brainstorm responses with a partner.

through the example of others. In our prayer life we are also affected by the history and experience of those who have lived before us. The Saints, as well as those who are living and praying today, are our mentors.

(CCC, 2653–2654)

Fed by the Word of God

As Christians venture further down their own spiritual path, fueled by their love for God, they uncover forms of prayer that are best suited for them. These ways of praying can be taught, learned, and implemented into a person's prayer life. A person realizes through practice and trial and error that some physical postures, some forms of prayer, are more suitable for them than other forms are.

Reading Sacred Scripture

The frequent reading of Sacred Scripture, the Word of God, is at the heart of our Christian tradition of prayer. Knowing how to read and then reading Sacred Scripture is a very important discipline that can be developed by practice. In prayer we engage in both a dialogue and an encounter with God. The prayerful reading of Sacred Scripture enriches and enlivens that dialogue and encounter. "The Holy Spirit gives a spiritual understanding of the Word of God to those who read or hear it, according to the dispositions of their hearts" (CCC, 1101).

By prayerfully reading Scripture, we develop a fuller understanding of the life and message of Jesus. We come to appreciate the struggle of his followers as they journeyed their spiritual path.

We deepen our understanding of the core truths and beliefs passed on to us by the apostles and early Christian writers. This is why the Bible is such an important source of sustenance for us.

By reading Sacred Scripture, we come to know Abraham, Moses, Miriam, Ruth, Isaiah, Jeremiah, Esther, and the faith stories of so many of our Old Testament ancestors. We are led into (and through) the Exodus of our own lives. Many of us overlook the extraordinary relationship that our Israelite ancestors had with God, and how that relationship helps us on our own spiritual journeys.

We also learn from the people of the New Testament. The stories of Mary, Peter, Nicodemus, and the Samaritan woman and others also help us understand the many dimensions of our prayer and spiritual lives. We learn from them and so many other believers how they forged their own course as they listened to and followed the voice of God.

We too, if we are to embark on a journey with the living God, will need to take the time to listen to the Spirit speaking to us through the sacred text of our faith—both the Old and the New Testaments. There we learn from the genuine struggle and searching of our ancestors in faith.

Meditating on Sacred Scripture

Our Catholic Tradition teaches us that the Bible is the inspired Word of God. The pages of the ancient and wise texts are not intended to be a mere social or political history. Rather the Word of God is an encounter—a life-changing encounter—with the living God and Spirit in our midst.

Meditating, or quietly reflecting, on Scripture with the desire to make God's Word our own deepens our communion with God in prayer.

Using our imagination and emotions, we ask the Spirit to help us not only to understand the Word of God but also to respond to what God is asking. The Bible then truly becomes for us the book of life.

FOR REFLECTION

In order to understand the power of prayer, we need to be fed through the wisdom of the Scriptures. In order to understand the wisdom of the Bible, we need to pray for insight.

· · · · Discuss:
What is your understanding of this statement?

Fed by the Liturgy of the Church

The Christian life of prayer is nourished also by the liturgy of the Church. It is through the sacramental liturgy of the Church that the mission of Christ and the Holy Spirit is proclaimed, made present, and proclaims the mystery of salvation. This is continued in the heart that prays. The liturgy is internalized by prayer. "Prayer is always prayer *of the Church;* it is a communion with the Holy Trinity" (CCC, 2655).

Joined with reading and meditating on Sacred Scripture, our participation in the **liturgy** of the Church is at the heart of our prayer life as Catholics. From the first days of the Church, it has been our tradition that through participating in the liturgy, the Spirit puts us into a "living relationship with Christ, the Word and Image of the Father, so that [we] can live out the meaning of what [we] hear, contemplate, and do in the celebration" (CCC, 1101).

Prayer—both personal and communal—shapes the way we live. Liturgical, or sacramental, prayer is at the center of our prayer life. It is preceded and followed by a broader life of prayer. We are reminded:

> The spiritual life, however, is not limited solely to participation in the liturgy. The Christian is indeed called to pray with others, but he must also enter into his bedroom to pray to his Father in secret (see Matthew 6:6); furthermore, according to the teaching of the apostle, he must pray without ceasing (see 1 Thessalonians 5:17).
>
> *Constitution on the Sacred Liturgy,* 12

Read and reflect on these passages from the Book of Psalms.

I waited, waited for the LORD;
who bent down and heard my cry.
Psalm 40:2

Oh, that today you would hear his voice:
Do not harden your hearts as at Meribah,
as on the day of Massah in the desert.
Psalm 95:7–8

Discuss:

What do these passages tell you about our posture, or attitude, when we pray? Share your insights with a partner.

Christians are people of prayer, living in communion with God—Father, Son, and Holy Spirit—present and active in our lives.

Prayer of the Church

By Baptism we are members of the Body of Christ. All Christian prayer, whether personal and "secret" or liturgical and "public," is the prayer of the Church. Our prayer is always made through, with, and in Christ together with the Holy Spirit. We truly never pray alone.

Too often we hear, "I don't like going to church; it's too boring and I don't get anything out of it." Rabbi Harold Kushner, in his book *Who Needs God,* talks of this phenomenon. His position is that we don't go to church to "get something out of it." We go to church to *give thanks to God* for the awesome opportunity to be alive, to be given the gift of love, of hope, of growth, of the presence of God.

If we go to church only to get something out of it, we might complain when the liturgy doesn't entertain us and keep our attention. We, then, don't go back. When this happens, we cut ourselves off from the nourishment and support of the community of believers. We cut ourselves off from a worshiping community where genuine spiritual nourishment can be shared and imparted. Our participation in the liturgy celebrates and nourishes our "communion," our life with God.

If we take part in the liturgy to give praise and thanks to God, we participate with a humble heart—with a totally selfless attitude, an attitude of surrender and graciousness.

(CCC, 2656–2658)

The Theological Virtues

God invites us to share in his life and love. The **Theological Virtues** of faith, hope, and love (charity) dispose Christians to live in communion with the Holy Trinity. These virtues, or powers, are given to us directly by God and give us the ability to live as children of God now and forever in eternal life (see CCC, 1812–1829).

Faith

By **faith** we freely commit ourselves to God (see *Dogmatic Constitution on Divine Revelation*). It is through the gate of *faith* that we can enter into prayer. Prayer without faith becomes empty. Through faith we dialogue with God, who is all-loving, all-powerful, all-knowing, always faithful, and full of mercy.

Hope

When our prayer flows from faith, it becomes the channel of trusting communication between ourselves and God. We pray in **hope.** Hope is the Theological Virtue by which we trust in Christ and the help of the Holy Spirit, our Advocate and Helper. It focuses our desire on the Kingdom of God and the promise of eternal happiness.

It is the Holy Spirit who teaches us to pray in hope. Our prayers become the avenue for hope. We trust that we will grow closer to the love of God and that we will be transformed by that love and fed by God's presence. Our prayer becomes rooted in trust, in a trust that God fulfills the promises made through

God in My Life

When we enter into a relationship with another person based on trust and love, we might evaluate how we are living that relationship by asking:

- How does this person treat me?

- What kinds of things does this person say about me?

- How am I becoming a better person through this relationship?

- In what ways am I getting along better with my family and friends?

- Does this relationship exclude everyone else from my life?

These are some of the questions we might ask ourselves to evaluate our relationship with another person. We can ask the same kinds of questions about our relationship with God.

· · · · Discuss:

Using these same questions, describe some of the ways your relationship with God manifests itself in your life.

Abraham, Moses, the prophets, and Jesus. We pray in hope because we believe and trust that:

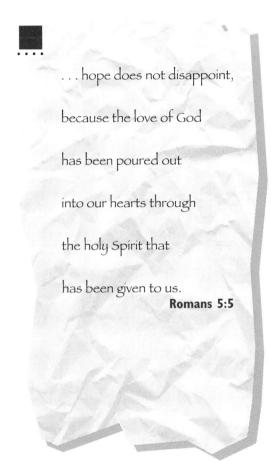

. . . hope does not disappoint,

because the love of God

has been poured out

into our hearts through

the holy Spirit that

has been given to us.

Romans 5:5

Love

Our prayer built on faith and hope opens us to the love, or **charity,** God pours into our hearts. We enter into a deeper, more trusting, more life-giving relationship with God, who is love (see 1 John 4:16). We experience and come to know that love is the source of true prayer.

(CCC, 2659–2660)

Praying Always

God is with us always. In "Footprints," which is found on page 11 of this book, the author struggled with coming to know and understand that God was present at all times in his or her life. One of the most essential insights to develop in our prayer life is to come to recognize God in every place, in every corner of our life. The Spirit of God is offered to us at all times, in the events of *each day,* to make prayer spring up from us—at the breakfast table, during math class, on stage during a performance, on the field during a competition.

Since God is always present with us, our life can be a life of prayer. "Time is in the Father's hands; it is in the present that we encounter him, not yesterday nor tomorrow, but today" (CCC, 2659). While sacred spaces, like a church, offer specific places for us to worship, they are not the only places where we can realize God's presence. God is present where we are, whether we are doing the dishes or kneeling to close our day.

We are encouraged "to pray always" by the writer of the Letter to the Hebrews. We are encouraged to bring "the help of prayer into humble, everyday situations" (CCC, 2660). It is not what we choose for words that matters nor the style of our posture that counts. It is our desire to encounter God where we are, at any given moment of our day, because God is "Emmanuel," God with us.

Prayer

❖ ❖ ❖

O God, who by the mystery of today's great feast sanctify your whole Church in every people and nation, pour out, we pray, the gifts of the Holy Spirit across the face of the earth and, with the divine grace that was at work when the Gospel was first proclaimed, fill now once more the hearts of believers.

Through our Lord Jesus Christ, your Son, who lives and reigns with you in the unity of the Holy Spirit, one God, for ever and ever. Amen.

COLLECT, PENTECOST SUNDAY, ROMAN MISSAL

REVIEW

IMPORTANT TERMS TO KNOW

charity—Theological Virtue; power to know and love and serve God above all else, and to love our neighbors as ourselves because of our love for God

faith—Theological Virtue that enables us to believe in God and what God has revealed through Scripture and the Church; God's invitation to believe and trust in him and our response to that invitation

hope—Theological Virtue; the power to trust in God and in his promises above everyone and everything else

liturgy—the Church worshiping God as a community. The word means "work of the people"; the liturgy is the work of the People of God, the Body of Christ, the Church.

Theological Virtues—faith, hope, and charity; bestowed at Baptism, these virtues have their origin and goal in God by relating us to the Holy Trinity.

CHAPTER SUMMARY

We all desire to know and love God better through prayer. Our prayer is nourished through the Holy Spirit, the Scriptures, and the liturgy. In this chapter we learned:

1. To pray well one must have the will to pray.

2. Made in the image and likeness of God, human beings have a natural hunger to know and love God.

3. The Holy Spirit is our guide; therefore it is proper to seek the direction of him in our prayer life.

4. Prayer should accompany the reading of Sacred Scripture, and the reading of Scripture should often accompany prayer.

5. Jesus Christ is at the center of our spirituality.

6. The liturgy of the Catholic Church is a rich and profound form of prayer and provides a solid source of nourishment for our spiritual lives.

7. One enters into prayer through the narrow gate of *faith,* which is best defined as "being in love with God."

8. Prayer nourishes hope in us, hope that we would continually grow closer to God and realize more fully God's love in our lives.

9. God is always present to us. Prayer opens us up to realize this presence. Therefore the more we pray, the more we are opening ourselves to the presence of God.

EXPLORING OUR CATHOLIC FAITH

1. Listening to God's Word

The psalm writer says,
"Oh, that today you would hear his voice:
    Do not harden your hearts"
(Psalm 95:7–8).
Reflect on specific ways that you can and will listen to God's voice today.

2. Understanding the Teachings of the Catholic Church

At the Second Vatican Council the bishops taught that Sacred Scripture serves "the children of the Church as strength for their faith, food for the soul, and a pure and lasting font of spiritual life" (*Constitution on Divine Revelation,* 25). Using this teaching of the Church, describe, in your own words, the importance of Sacred Scripture in the prayer life of Christians.

3. Reflecting on Our Catholic Faith

Saint Jerome wrote, "Ignorance of the Scriptures is ignorance of Christ" (*Commentary on Isaiah).* How does this insight help you to grow as a person of prayer? Write your thoughts in your journal.

4. Living Our Catholic Faith

To grow as a person of prayer, we must practice, practice, practice. With several friends, draw up a list of things you could practice to grow as people of prayer.

CHAPTER 6

The Way of Prayer

I love the LORD, who listened
to my voice in supplication,
Who turned an ear to me
on the day I called.

PSALM 116:1–2

Read and reflect on the statement. Tell whether you agree or disagree with it.

The language of prayer has many dimensions: words, melodies, gestures, and so on.

The morning bell rings, but to the rest of the world it is still the middle of the night. Brother Sebastian rises and puts on his long gray robe in silence.

The only sound is the squeak of sandals on the stone corridors as he joins the other **monks** on the way to the oratory. The chapel is soon filled with the vibrant and reverberating sound of chanting voices. Throughout the day Brother Sebastian will join the others in the monastery six times to chant the praises of the Lord. Their whole day is determined by the hours of prayer—and not by the hours of the clock.

KEY TERMS

icon

invocation

mantra

monk

Psalter

Rosary

What are some of the ways you pray?

Which events in your day call you to pray?

Brother Sebastian and the monks had a disciplined prayer life. Their schedule of prayer helped them focus throughout the day on their relationship with God. All other tasks and relationships were placed within their relationship with God.

The life of daily prayer of the monks included chanting the **Psalter,** kneeling and bowing, sitting, and other ways of praying that have come to be known as monastic prayer. While the way of prayer of Brother Sebastian and the monks had its own unique style, the heart of their prayer was similar to that of all Christians. In this chapter we will explore the way of Christian prayer, which includes prayer to the Father, to Jesus, to the Holy Spirit, and to the Virgin Mary.

> [**T**]here are as many paths of prayer as there are persons who pray, but it is the same Spirit acting in all and with all.
>
> CCC, 2672

(Catechism of the Catholic Church, 2663)

The Living Tradition of Prayer

Christian prayer is a living tradition. There are many ways the people of God authentically express their prayer. Christian prayer has a history; it has developed and continues to develop within the historical, social, and cultural context of people. It is expressed verbally and nonverbally,

with the language of people. "The Magisterium of the Church (see *Constitution on Divine Revelation,* 10) has the task of discerning the fidelity of these ways of praying to the tradition of apostolic faith" (CCC, 2663).

Words, Signs, and Symbolic Actions

Christian prayer includes a mixture of signs and symbols. As humans we communicate with one another verbally and nonverbally. We combine words, gestures, and symbolic actions that express more fully the meaning of what we wish to communicate. The same is necessarily true of our communication with God, with our prayer.

These words, gestures, and actions are part of the culture and society within which we live. Rooted in human nature and creation, they express the mystery of God's work among us, revealed in the events of the Old Covenant and especially in Christ, the New Covenant, and his Paschal Mystery. The use of water, for example, symbolizes both life and death. Burning incense gives expression to our belief that our prayers rise to God and are heard. The lighting of candles symbolizes the nearness of God, dwelling in our midst. Kneeling in prayer expresses our dependence on God while standing witnesses to our respect for God, who is present with us.

Singing and Music

Song and music have always been part of the prayer life of the People of God. From the song of Miriam, to the psalms of David, to the canticles and hymns of the New Testament, the prayer of the People of God has always been expressed through song and music.

The Church has always supported the fine arts and their use in Christian prayer. The Church through the Second Vatican Council teaches:

> The fine arts are rightly classed among the noblest activities of man's genius; this is especially true of religious art and of its highest manifestation, sacred art. Of their nature the arts are directed toward expressing in some way the infinite beauty of God in works made by human hands. Their dedication to the increase of God's praise and of his glory is more complete, the more exclusively they are devoted to turning men's minds devoutly toward God.
>
> *Constitution on the Sacred Liturgy*, 122

Discuss: What role do music and art play in your prayer life? In the life of your parish community?

The importance and role of music in Christian prayer is clearly stated by the Church. In the *Constitution on the Sacred Liturgy,* the Church teaches:

> The musical tradition of the universal Church is a treasure of inestimable value, greater even than that of any other art. . . . The treasury of sacred music is to be preserved and cultivated with great care (112, 114).

Art, Sacred Images, and Iconography

God chose to make himself visible to us in the sending of his Son, who became flesh and lived among us. In Jesus, in his person and in his works, God revealed himself to us in human form.

Christians, likewise, throughout the centuries have created **icons** and sacred images to remind themselves of the mystery of God's work among us. "The beauty of the images moves me to contemplation," wrote Saint John Damascene. The Church's teaching on the place and meaning of Christian art and images is stated in the *Catechism:* "Christian iconography expresses in images the same Gospel message that Scripture communicates by words" (CCC, 1160).

The Spirit guides the Church to a deeper relationship with God in Jesus through its life of prayer. It is the task of the Magisterium to listen to and discern the proddings of the Holy Spirit. It is the role of pastors and religious educators to explain the many dimensions of the Christian journey of prayer.

The Journey to God: The Way of Prayer

We are invited to freely give of ourselves to God. At the heart of the human person is the presence of God. After all, we are made in the image and likeness of our Creator. Inasmuch as we respond to the presence of God in every corner of our lives, we open ourselves up to God's mercy, compassion, forgiveness, and love. As we become more aware of and respond to God working in and among the events of our lives, we are transformed, little by little, into who we are and what we have been created to be: images of God, children of God.

Prayer to the Father

Christian prayer, like the prayer of Christ, is, above all, prayer to God the Father. When his disciples asked Jesus to teach them to pray, he responded:

> "When you pray, say:
> Father, hallowed be your name,
> your kingdom come."
>
> Luke 11:2

United to Christ through our baptism, we are one with him. In Christ, we receive every blessing and gift from God. In him and through him and with him the Spirit teaches us to pray. "We ask this through our Lord Jesus Christ, your Son," we pray, "who lives and reigns with you and the Holy Spirit, one God, for ever and ever."

Jesus is the way to the Father. It is in his name we pray. "And whatever you ask in my name, I will do, so that the Father may be glorified in the Son. If you ask anything of me in my name," he promised, "I will do it" (John 14:13–14). "There is no other way of Christian prayer than Christ" (CCC, 2664).

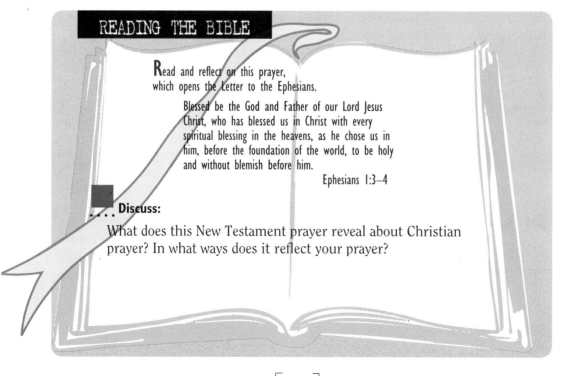

READING THE BIBLE

Read and reflect on this prayer, which opens the Letter to the Ephesians.

Blessed be the God and Father of our Lord Jesus Christ, who has blessed us in Christ with every spiritual blessing in the heavens, as he chose us in him, before the foundation of the world, to be holy and without blemish before him.

Ephesians 1:3–4

Discuss:

What does this New Testament prayer reveal about Christian prayer? In what ways does it reflect your prayer?

Prayer to Jesus

Our prayer is "in the name of" Jesus: the Son of God, Word of God, Savior, and Lord, who is our resurrection and our life. In his name is our Salvation.

While Christian prayer is primarily addressed to the Father, our tradition of both liturgical and personal prayer includes praying not only in the name of Jesus but also to Jesus. It has been the faith of the Church, since its very first days, that whoever calls upon the "name of the Lord" will be saved (see Romans 10:13).

To pray the name of "Jesus" is to bless and praise God for all he is and has done for us.

The Jesus Prayer. The Jesus Prayer— "Lord Jesus Christ, Son of God, have mercy on us, sinners"—is a simple, prayerful expression of our faith. It speaks of our faith in God's love and mercy for us that is revealed in Jesus, especially in the Paschal Mystery of his Death, Resurrection, and Ascension.

Said over and over again, it becomes an **invocation,** or a beautiful **mantra.** It continually reminds us of the love of God and keeps us aware of the presence of that love with us right now.

The Jesus Prayer reminds us that our prayer need not be complex, using complicated forms and sophisticated language. The prayer of our heart is more important than the prayer of our lips. God knows our hearts and hears even when we do not speak. Our words are not as important as our desire to come to God, bearing ourselves as the gift to him.

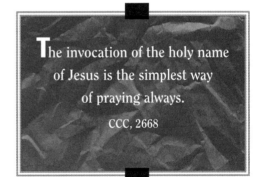

The invocation of the holy name of Jesus is the simplest way of praying always.

CCC, 2668

Prayer to the Holy Spirit

The Spirit of God "is the artisan of the living tradition of prayer" (CCC, 2672). In writing to the Church in Corinth, Paul teaches, "[N]o one can say, 'Jesus is Lord,' except by the holy Spirit" (1 Corinthians 12:3).

The Holy Spirit is "the interior Master of Christian prayer" (CCC, 2672). Christian prayer to the Father is made through Christ, with Christ, in Christ, in the unity of the Holy Spirit (see *Roman Missal,* Eucharistic Prayer). It is the Spirit who invites us to pray and teaches us what to say. That is why we call upon the Spirit:

Come Holy Spirit, fill the hearts of your faithful and enkindle in them the fire of your love.

Roman Missal, Pentecost

(CCC, 2673–2679)

Prayer to and in Communion with Mary

Mary, the mother of Jesus, is our mother too. From the Annunciation to the Death of Jesus, to the coming of the Spirit on Pentecost, Mary shows us the way of prayer. She is the perfect pray-er. Filled with the Spirit and united with her son, her prayer is always a prayer of faith and trust.

As members of the Body of Christ, the Communion of Saints, we unite ourselves in prayer with Mary and all the faithful, living and dead. We pray with her and to her.

The Hail Mary

The Hail Mary is a beautiful and ancient prayer of the Church. It embraces the kind of humility that we seek when we approach God in prayer. This prayer offers us wonderful insight into both the profound relationship that Mary had with God and the gracious spiritual posture she had. It may help to break open the prayer in a way that sheds light on its meaning.

Hail, Mary. The greeting that the angel Gabriel uses opens this prayer. God greets Mary personally, and Mary humbly enters the presence of God.

Full of grace, the Lord is with thee. Mary is full of grace because God is always with her, intimately related to her. Mary is filled with the grace from the source of all grace because she has fully opened her heart to God and completely given herself over to God in faith, hope, and love.

Blessed art thou among women and blessed is the fruit of thy womb, Jesus. Mary is blessed because of her faith and her complete surrender to the will of God. She is the mother of the Son of God; the "fruit of her womb" is Jesus. For this reason is she "blessed among women." And for these reasons we honor her place in the whole of Salvation History.

Holy Mary, Mother of God. "And how does this happen to me," Elizabeth greets Mary, "that the mother of my Lord should come to me?" (Luke 1:43). As Mary is the Mother of God, the Church teaches us that she is our mother too. She is holy because of who she is and because she is the mother of Jesus. "By entrusting ourselves to her prayer, we abandon ourselves to the will of God together with her" (CCC, 2677).

Pray for us sinners, now and at the hour of our death. By asking Mary to pray for us, we are acknowledging that we are her children. In this last part of the prayer we give ourselves to her, imperfect and striving for holiness as we may be. We trust that she will pray on our behalf to God our Creator, even "at the hour of our death."

The Rosary

During medieval times the prayer of the **Rosary** was developed as a prayer to be said throughout the day. It enabled Christians to reflect upon God's love for them, revealed in the mysteries of Christ's life. From this time onward the Church has regarded this prayer with great respect. Prayed well and reflectively, the Rosary provides a beautiful window to the presence of God in our lives.

A powerful image of Mary is that of the Pieta, by Michelangelo, which is now in Saint Peter's Basilica in Rome. Imagine what Mary must have been feeling and thinking as she held the body of her son in her arms.

. . . . Discuss:
Reflect on the pain that Mary must have felt as she held the limp, lifeless body of her son after watching him die a criminal's death on the Cross.

Prayer

❖ ❖ ❖

A litany is a prayer, part of which is meant to be repeated. The repetition so draws the pray-ers into the rhythm that they are caught up into the prayer. Pray these selected verses from the Litany of the Holy Name.

Lord, have mercy
    Lord, have mercy
Christ, have mercy
    Christ, have mercy
Lord, have mercy
    Lord, have mercy

God our Father in heaven
    have mercy on us
God the Son, Redeemer of the world
    have mercy on us
God the Holy Spirit
    have mercy on us
Holy Trinity, one God
    have mercy on us

Jesus, Son of the living God
    have mercy on us
Jesus, Son of the Virgin Mary
    have mercy on us
Jesus, prince of peace
    have mercy on us
Jesus, Good Shepherd
    have mercy on us
Jesus, courage of martyrs
    have mercy on us

Lord, be merciful
    Jesus, save your people
By the mystery of your Incarnation
    Jesus, save your people
By your death and burial
    Jesus, save your people
By your rising to new life
    Jesus, save your people
By your return in glory to the Father
    Jesus, save your people.

From *Catholic Household Blessings and Prayers*

REVIEW

IMPORTANT TERMS TO KNOW

icon—a sacred image, especially a painted image of Jesus, Mary, or a saint used in the liturgy and decoration of Eastern churches

invocation—a short prayer—a word or phrase—that is repeated slowly, over and over again; an invocation is similar to a mantra

mantra—a form of invocation, an incantation that enables a person to enter into the rhythm of prayer

monk—one who professes and lives a form of religious life that includes professing the vows of poverty, chastity, and obedience, and living according to a rule of life either in community or alone

Psalter—a book containing the psalms and other hymns and canticles that are found in Sacred Scripture and used in the celebration of the Church's liturgy

Rosary—prayer honoring Mary in which we remember the saving events, or mysteries, in the life of Jesus and Mary

CHAPTER SUMMARY

The Catholic tradition of prayer includes many different ways to pray. In this chapter we learned:

1. Prayer is primarily addressed to God the Father.

2. Christian prayer is also addressed to Christ. "The invocation of the holy name of Jesus is the simplest way of praying always" (CCC, 2667).

3. We also call upon the Spirit in prayer. No one can say "Jesus is Lord" unless the Holy Spirit guides them. It is the Holy Spirit who invites us and empowers us to pray. The Holy Spirit is "the interior Master of Christian prayer" (CCC, 2672).

4. Because of her unique and holy role in the plan of Salvation, we join with Mary in prayer and call on her to intercede for us in prayer.

EXPLORING OUR CATHOLIC FAITH

1. Listening to God's Word

Christians have always prayed the psalms. A psalm is a prayer song. Look up and page through the Book of Psalms in the Old Testament. Notice both the many different moods of the psalmist and the many types of psalms. Choose one or several psalms to pray. How do they help you express yourself to God in prayer?

2. Understanding the Teachings of the Catholic Church

The *Catechism* teaches that "there are as many paths of prayer as there are persons who pray, but it is the same Spirit acting in all and with all" (CCC, 2672). Discuss how your prayer is different from that of your friends. Find the similarities in the way the Spirit works with your prayer and in the prayer of your friends.

3. Reflecting on Our Catholic Faith

Saint Ignatius said, "Even the desire to be closer to God does in fact draw us closer to God." What does this say to you about wanting to get closer to God through prayer? Write your reflections in your journal.

4. Living Our Catholic Faith

Spend some time in quiet, praying the Jesus Prayer.

CHAPTER 7

Guides for Prayer along the Way

Pray without ceasing.

1 THESSALONIANS 5:17

What questions about your life do you have most difficulty finding answers to?

What questions do you have most difficulty talking about?

John, you just have to read this article!" Marcia exclaimed as she shoved a paper into John's face. They had been friends for the last three years of high school and had developed a close relationship. Each one felt comfortable talking together about all the issues in their lives.

"I thought immediately of you and some of the questions you've been having about God. This might not really *answer* your questions, but it may help you."

John just shook his head. "I don't think anyone has the answers to *my* questions. Sometimes it feels empty inside, like when I pray I feel it's just words that fill the air, going nowhere."

Marcia wished she knew the right thing to say. "Just read the article. It might give you another way to look at your questions."

How have other people helped you answer difficult questions in your life?

KEY TERMS

Blessed Sacrament

Divine Office

Liturgy of the Hours

pilgrimage

spiritual director

John's questions are not uncommon; in fact, they are universal. To lead a truly human life, we need to develop a spirituality. This means we need to develop and live a way of life that is designed around our response to the Spirit.

All of us are born with a hunger for God. In each corner, at every junction of our life, God stands with us and invites us into relationship with him. The challenge of the spiritual journey is to become open to and to respond to that divine presence. In this chapter we will explore the reality that we do not stand alone or travel our spiritual journey alone.

(*Catechism of the Catholic Church*, 2683–2684)

Companions

Each of us stands at a different place on our spiritual journey. Each of us has different needs and desires, different gifts and abilities. But God invites each of us—where we are, as we are—to live in communion with him and with one another.

Basic Questions

Many of us sometimes stand bewildered, with a look of confusion on our faces. We ask:

❑ What is God asking me to do?
❑ How will I respond to God's invitation? What will I need to give up in order to accept that gift?
❑ What will be the sacrifices?
❑ How many strings are attached?
❑ If I respond, if I accept the offer, who will support me?
❑ Since Jesus promised and sent the Spirit and never intended for us to journey alone, who will be our companions along the way?

These are important questions. They help frame our understanding of the mystery of God. They shape how we look at God and at ourselves in relationship to God and to one another. We need to seek out answers to these questions. This is why it is so important for us to seek the advice, counsel, wisdom, and experience of others.

Seeking Advice

Whether it is confiding in our parents, our parish priest, or our favorite teacher; whether it is studying the teachings and traditions of the Catholic Church or the writings of such great spiritual leaders as Saint John of the Cross, Saint Teresa of Ávila (Teresa of Jesus), Blessed Julian of Norwich, or others, it is necessary to *listen* to the experience of others. If we are to grow in deeper understanding and awareness of the presence of God in our lives, we need to learn from those who are wiser than we are. We need to listen to those who not only have asked questions similar to ours but also, who, through prayer and faith, have discovered answers that have given them the vision and strength to live their life in Christ.

> We need to pray first for open minds and open hearts, for hearts of flesh rather than of stone.

A Cloud of Witnesses

We need to be attentive to the many people of faith who have traveled their spiritual journey before us. They are part of God's gift to us. Relying on our own vision (or lack of vision) will allow us to travel a limited distance. Only with the aid of others can we expand our understanding, our horizons, and our vision. Who are some of these people?

Saints. The Saints are those people who have been recognized by the Church community to have lived lives that were profound examples of their love for God. The Saints are people who gave their lives to the will and purpose that God made known to them. These were people who lived extraordinary lives of commitment and conviction. They were children and adults, those who lived in poverty and those who were born into wealth; they were farmers, lawyers, teachers, and kings. They were people like you and me, who came from all walks of life.

Some of them died the death of a hero, standing up for faith in God. They lived to the last breath a faith that fueled their visions and drove their desire to know and love God more deeply each day.

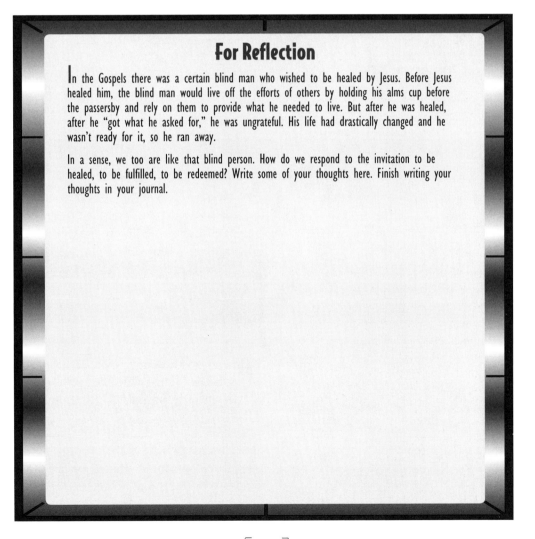

For Reflection

In the Gospels there was a certain blind man who wished to be healed by Jesus. Before Jesus healed him, the blind man would live off the efforts of others by holding his alms cup before the passersby and rely on them to provide what he needed to live. But after he was healed, after he "got what he asked for," he was ungrateful. His life had drastically changed and he wasn't ready for it, so he ran away.

In a sense, we too are like that blind person. How do we respond to the invitation to be healed, to be fulfilled, to be redeemed? Write some of your thoughts here. Finish writing your thoughts in your journal.

Reading and listening to God's Word can be full of surprises. Ours is a God of surprises. God often reveals himself as one who defies human logic. The parables were a way for Jesus to offer us a glimpse of the illogical, incomprehensible, yet lovingly intimate God. Read and reflect on Matthew 13:1–9, the parable of the Sower and the Seed.

Discuss:

In your life, who represents the sower?

Who or what are the weeds?

What are the rocks in your life?

What was the task of the sower?

What is our task?

In what ways do you think the parable is about our spiritual lives?

From the lives of the Saints come various examples of spiritualities on which we can model our own. In the midst of our own questioning, the Saints provide for us signposts that we can follow on our own journeys.

The Catholic Church is a community rich in spiritual wisdom. Everywhere we look, whether in the events of the present or in the roots of our past, we can find examples and models of people whose lives are focused on God and on living the Great Commandment. Ours is a rich spiritual tradition that is as diverse as the many people who have walked its

(CCC, 2685–2690)

Servants of Prayer

Prayer is our communion with God. It is the living relationship we have with the Holy Trinity and the foundation of our spirituality. Yet, while we believe that praying should be as constant and "natural" to us as breathing, we know that we need to learn how to pray. Who can we turn to for help?

The Christian Family

The Catholic Church has always taught that the family is the primary source of Christian education. It has always been the domestic Church—the place where God's children learn Christian prayer and spirituality. Within the lived faith of parents, children come to know the love of God. The family is the first witness of the presence of God living among us.

Ordained Ministers

Ordained ministers have the vocation and responsibility for the growth of the People of God, the Church. They preside over the liturgy; they teach us about our faith and lead us in living lives of faith, hope, and charity. Through proclaiming and preaching the Word of God, they lead us to discern God at work in our lives.

Religious Orders

Many men and women dedicate their whole lives to prayer. Hermits, monks, and nuns, since the time of the desert fathers, have lived in solitude or joined with others to live in a community devoted to prayer—to praising God and interceding for the needs of his people.

Today, many men and women keep the Church's tradition of contemplative prayer. They live in prayerful silence and contemplation. Their prayer is one of complete surrender, and their lives are a complete commitment to the spiritual needs of the world.

Catechists

Catechesis is the teaching and passing on of the beliefs and the religious and spiritual traditions of the Church. In catechesis, children, young people, and

---

SCHOOLS OF SPIRITUALITY

The spiritual vision of many of the Saints lives on in their followers. It has become a way of life for them. Research and briefly describe the spiritual vision of each of these Saints. Then list some of the aspects of the spirituality for which it is the foundation.

Saint Basil (c. 329–379)

Saint Benedict (480–c. 546)

Saint Teresa of Ávila
(Teresa of Jesus) (1515–1582)

Blessed Julian of Norwich
(c. 1342–c. 1420)

Saint Thérèse of Lisieux (Thérèse of the Child Jesus) (1873–1897)

---

adults are invited not only to study the teachings of the Church but also to meditate on the Word of God in personal prayer. In teaching these basic beliefs and practices of the Church, catechists help build within their learners a foundation for further study, insight, and knowledge about the richness of our Catholic faith.

Prayer Groups

Since the Second Vatican Council, prayer groups have become more common in the life of the Church. From charismatic communities to small home-based groups, Christians gather in prayer to support and encourage one another in living their lives in Christ. These "schools of prayer" (CCC, 2689) witness to the growing desire of Christians to commit themselves to search for a deeper relationship with God in Christ in their daily lives.

Prayer groups provide a wellspring of authentic Christian spirituality and prayer. They reflect our belief that Christians are genuinely a community of believers who share a common journey with Christ and the Spirit that is fueled by a common hunger for God. The way we know the genuine nature of a Catholic prayer group is whether it reflects the teachings of the Catholic Church.

Spiritual Directors

The saying "You can't see the forest for the trees" reflects the idea that often we are so close to something that we cannot see or appreciate it. This saying also applies to our spiritual lives. We often find ourselves praying, doing all the things we think are necessary to attain a deeper faith, but we don't seem to be going anywhere. These are the times when we need someone else who can help us see clearer—someone with the insight to discern the workings of the Holy Spirit in our lives.

The Catholic Church teaches that the Holy Spirit bestows gifts on all the faithful. To some are given the gifts of "wisdom, faith and discernment for the sake of this common good which is prayer" (CCC, 2690). We call such a person a **spiritual director.** A spiritual director is a person who is aware of the dimensions of the spiritual life and journey and who has been on her or his own faith journey for a long period

of time. A spiritual director is someone whom we can trust and who helps us see beyond the yearning of our own hearts, beyond the limits of our own wisdom. He or she helps us see what we do not see or, for some reason, refuse to see.

(CCC, 2691)

Places Favorable for Prayer

Each of us also needs to discover surroundings that help us meet God in prayer. When we go about the task of praying, it is important to find a place, or places, that are conducive to prayer.

A Personal Prayer Space

A personal prayer space helps us meet God in the private moments of our lives, within the secret of our own hopes and desires. One person might set aside space in their bedroom, for example in a corner, with a Bible, a candle and some sacred object, while another person may seek the quiet comfort of the woods. Yet others may find it helpful to listen to instrumental music that sparks the imagination with sacred visions.

While the presence of God dwells within every human heart, it is our task to make ourselves receptive to that presence in order that we might recognize God in every corner of our lives. Setting a place apart, away from the confusion of our lives, is a wonderful way to express our desire to know and love God, and to respond to his presence with us.

Church

Throughout the centuries, our church buildings have been places for us to focus on God's presence with us. When we enter a church, we temporarily step away from the mainstream of our daily lives. There we meet and visit with God.

Visiting a church and praying before the **Blessed Sacrament** is unique to Catholicism. We place ourselves before Christ, really and sacramentally present with us. We avail ourselves of a wonderful opportunity to reflect on and be blessed by God.

Monasteries and Convents

The Spirit invites us to pray constantly (see 1 Thessalonians 5:17). In chapter 6, we reflected on how the daily life of Brother Sebastian and the monks was marked by the rhythm of prayer. Today, the ordained ministers of the Church and men and women religious carry on this tradition of "praying constantly" by praying the **Liturgy of the Hours,** or the **Divine Office,** as a community in their monasteries or convents.

The Liturgy of the Hours is the prayer of the whole People of God. So important is this tradition for the life of the Church that many parishes call people together in the morning and evening to pray Morning Prayer or Evening Prayer, which are part of the Liturgy of the Hours. Still within our reach and locale there exists a wonderful opportunity to participate more fully in the prayer of the Church, the Liturgy of the Hours. This is a beautiful prayer that calls upon God with the Psalms, the Old Testament and New Testament Scriptures, and the prayers of our living Catholic Tradition.

Pilgrimages

Our whole life is a **pilgrimage**—a spiritual journey with God. Pilgrimages nourish us in a special way for that journey. They are "special occasions for renewal in prayer. For pilgrims seeking living water, shrines are special places for living the forms of Christian prayer 'in Church'" (CCC, 2691).

Prayer

❖ ❖ ❖

We are people of prayer called to pray constantly. It is the Holy Spirit who invites us to pray and to make our life's journey with God.

Come, Holy Spirit, come!
And from your celestial home
　Shed a ray of light divine!

O most blessed Light divine,
Shine within these hearts of yours,
　And our inmost being fill!

Heal our wounds, our strength renew;
On our dryness pour your dew;
　Wash the stains of guilt away:

Bend the stubborn heart and will;
Melt the frozen, warm the chill;
　Guide the steps that go astray.

On the faithful, who adore
And confess you, evermore
　In your sevenfold gift descend;

Give them virtue's sure reward;
Give them your salvation, Lord;
　Give the joys that never end. Amen.
　Alleluia.

FROM *LECTIONARY*, PENTECOST SEQUENCE

REVIEW

IMPORTANT TERMS TO KNOW

Blessed Sacrament—the sacramental presence of Jesus Christ in the bread and wine at the altar, and reserved in the tabernacle

Divine Office—another name for the Liturgy of the Hours

Liturgy of the Hours—the official public prayer of the Church in which Christ united with his Body gives praise to God throughout the day. It includes the Office of Readings, Morning Prayer, Daytime Prayer, Evening Prayer, and Night Prayer.

pilgrimage—a journey to a religious place or holy person, based on one's belief in God's presence at the place or with the person

spiritual director—a person recognized by the Church to serve as a companion and guide to help others understand their relationship with God and their spiritual journey

CHAPTER SUMMARY

As Christians we are on a spiritual journey with God in Christ. Led by the Spirit we journey in many ways. In this chapter we learned:

1. We join ourselves with the communion of saints in prayer.

2. There are different schools of Christian spirituality. Each has much to offer us as we continue to uncover and discover the presence of God in our lives.

3. The Christian family is the first place for religious education and the first model in prayer.

4. Ordained ministers, religious communities, religious educators (catechists), prayer groups, and spiritual directors guide us in the practice of prayer on our spiritual journey.

5. The most appropriate places of prayer are personal or family spaces, monasteries, places of pilgrimage, and churches.

6. The Liturgy of the Hours is the prayer of the Body of Christ, head and members, giving praise to God throughout the day.

EXPLORING OUR CATHOLIC FAITH

1. Listening to God's Word

Read Matthew 6:6 and reflect on what it says about private prayer. Discuss the meaning of this for your life. Contrast it with praying in a public place.

2. Understanding the Teachings of the Catholic Church

Share with others how you learned to pray in your family. What were your first experiences of prayer? What prayer traditions do you continue now?

3. Reflecting on Our Catholic Faith

Thomas Merton said, "But I believe that the desire to please you does in fact please you." How do you desire to please God? Spend some time in prayer, talking to God about your desire to please him.

4. Living Our Catholic Faith

Most journeys go better with a companion. Who are some of the people who could help you on your journey? In your journal write a "job description" for your personal spiritual companion. Select a spiritual director and consult with him or her often.

CHAPTER 8

The Life of Prayer

They devoted themselves
to the teaching of the apostles
and to the communal life,
to the breaking of the bread
and to the prayers.

ACTS 2:42

What Do You Think?

Describe what you mean by prayer.

Name your favorite prayers.

What is the way you most like to pray?

In his play *Long Day's Journey into Night,* Eugene O'Neill has Edmund describe a mystical experience. Actually, it was one that O'Neill himself had one night on a square-rigger bound for Buenos Aires: "For a moment, I lost myself. . . . I became the white sails and flying spray, became the beauty and the rhythm, became the moonlight and the ship and the dim-starred sky! I belonged . . . within something greater than my own life. . . . To God if you want."

KEY TERMS

acedia

contemplation

liturgical year

meditation

spiritual reading

vocal prayer

When have you had an experience similar to O'Neill's?

Would you consider O'Neill's experience an experience of prayer? Why or why not?

Prayer for most of us begins as something that we have to make a conscious effort to do, but praying needs to grow into something more. It becomes as natural as breathing. It becomes a life source for us. In this chapter we will explore various types of prayer.

(Catechism of the Catholic Church, 2697–2699)

The Rhythm of Prayer

Scripture tells us that we ought to "pray without ceasing." But this is impossible unless we begin to pray at specific times, consciously choosing to do so. We need to develop a rhythm of prayer that is as natural to us as breathing. The life of prayer of the Church community provides us with opportunities to make prayer a natural part of our life. Here are some of those opportunities.

Daily Prayer

In order to develop a rhythm of prayer, we must pray, and pray regularly. This includes dedicating time each day for prayer as the Church does in the praying of the Liturgy of the Hours. Our daily life provides many natural, seemingly obvious moments for prayer.

Praying in the morning helps us focus on the day and God's presence with us. The morning provides an opportunity to reflect on what kind of person we will bring to our world. Praying between classes or during a free time of the day or at mealtimes keeps us in rhythm. At midday we can pause to see if we are still on the way. Praying at the end of the day allows us to give thanks to

God. At eventide we can look back and reflect on the grace that touched our lives as well as the times we were a channel of grace to others. In order to go from not praying to praying always, we have to start somewhere—we need to find the rhythm of the Spirit, who lives within us, guiding and helping us.

Eucharistic Prayer

For Christians Sunday is the sabbath, the Lord's Day. The Lord's Supper, the Eucharist, is its center. It is the time we gather to pray as the Body of Christ. We listen to the Word of God and share in the Eucharist. The Eucharist is the heart of our Christian life of prayer. The other Sacraments and all prayer flow from it and toward it. Without taking part in the Eucharist, our prayer life is out of rhythm.

Liturgical Year

Throughout the year the Church remembers and celebrates the Paschal Mystery of Christ—God's saving presence among us in Christ. At the heart of the **liturgical year** of the Church is the Easter Triduum, the celebration of the Death-Resurrection of Jesus. All other seasons and feasts unfold this great mystery of our faith and enable us to share in it. The liturgical year helps us participate in a cycle, or rhythm, that orchestrates our prayer life throughout the year.

> **W**e must remember God more often than we draw breath.
>
> SAINT GREGORY OF NAZIANZUS

The liturgical year is made up of a cycle of seasons and feasts. These create a rhythm that helps us recall and share in the mystery of God's saving love so that these are made present for all time. Think about these seasons and feasts. How do they create a rhythm for your prayer life? How do they help you share in God's saving love?

Annunciation

Advent

Christmas

Epiphany

Lent

Easter Triduum: Holy Thursday, Good Friday, Easter Vigil, Easter Sunday

Easter

Pentecost

Expressions of Prayer

In addition to offering us a pattern or rhythm to our life of prayer, our Christian tradition teaches us that there are three main expressions of prayer. They are vocal prayer, meditation, and contemplation. The one dimension that each has in common with the other is the honest opening of our heart and our attentive listening to God.

Vocal Prayer

God speaks to us through his Word. "In the beginning was the Word," the Gospel of John begins, "and the Word was with God, and the Word was God" (John 1:1).

Vocal prayer is the expression of our prayer in words. Words are powerful symbols. Through them we communicate who we are—we name our feelings, our thoughts, our deepest desires. There is also a certain mystery about words. They are symbolic and often are packed with meaning not clearly understood and not always recognized by others.

Vocal prayer is given shape through words, either spoken aloud or silently in our minds. However, the most important thing that we bring to vocal prayer—and all expressions of prayer—is not so much the words we speak but rather the attitude of our heart and our presence before God. True vocal prayer depends not so much on the number of words but on the fervor of our hearts.

Even though God knows our hearts before we speak, the words we use are useful more for us in naming and identifying our wants and needs, our joys and sorrows, as we bring their realities before our God.

We are both body and spirit. We have a natural desire and need to communicate our experiences, especially those that transform us. When Willy falls in love with Kelly, his most natural instinct is to talk about it, to share it with others. If you were Willy's best friend, you would probably hear more about Kelly than you ever wanted to know. Willy wants to tell people of the great discovery that has "transformed" his life.

The very same thing happens when we experience the love of God. We desire to share it—to talk about it, to give our experience definition and shape. Our prayer rises from the depths of our soul. What we come to know in our inner life we express externally. Words help us do that.

The Prayer of Meditation

The second traditional expression of Christian prayer is **meditation.** The prayer of meditation goes beyond the use of words and engages our thought, imagination, emotion, and desire. In meditation the Spirit leads us to reflect, in the quiet of our lives, on the mystery of God present with us so that we might *respond* to his voice. In this sense, the prayer of meditation is a quest, a searching, the expression of our desire to do God's will. Through meditation we reflect on the mysteries of Jesus Christ. We come to know God's love for us and respond, as Jesus did, by making that love known to others by what we say and do.

The Gospels pass on to us many examples of Jesus praying aloud to his Father. Prayerfully read and reflect on these Gospel passages. Describe what Jesus is expressing to his Father.

Matthew 11:25–26

John 17:1–26

Mark 14:36

Matthew 27:46

My Prayer

Think about the relationships and events that are an important part of your life. Ask the Spirit to help you share them with the Father as Jesus did.

. . . . Methods of Meditation . . . .

The prayer of meditation is facilitated through the reading of Sacred Scripture, the use of sacred images, icons and other sacred objects, and **spiritual reading.**

Scripture. When we read Sacred Scripture, we might imagine ourselves to be one of the followers of Jesus within a Gospel story. This can bring that story to life and help us visualize our relationship with Jesus. For example, imagining ourselves to be Martha or Mary, Zacchaeus, or one of the disciples in the boat being battered by the waves can help us open our hearts to Jesus and deepen our faith and trust in God.

Sacred Images. Meditating before a crucifix can help us come to know the depth of God's love for us and inspire us to proclaim and share that love with others. Francis of Assisi knelt in meditation before the crucifix in the village church of San Damiano in his desire to know what God was asking of him. During that prayer of meditation, he began to realize that he had the mission to "rebuild the Church." Afire with God's love, he left that moment of meditation and gave his life in pursuit of that work.

Prayer of Meditation

Take a moment and practice the prayer of meditation. Follow these simple steps.

1. Choose a Gospel passage. Slowly and prayerfully read it. Which person or people in the story do you identify with?

2. Imagine you are that person. Pause often and take time to become one with that person and the story.

3. Think about what in the story speaks to you most. Why is that? What feelings or emotions does it evoke?

4. Express your thoughts and feelings to God.

5. Open your mind and heart. Remember you are in God's presence. Listen for God's response.

6. Make God's response part of your life.

Spiritual Reading. The reading of books, poems, and essays by acknowledged spiritual writers is also very helpful in our quest for God. What we read confronts us, challenges us, forces us to make choices and drives us deeper into the heart of God. To the extent that we are humble and to the extent that we are faithful to our journey, we discover that spiritual reading stirs our hearts and moves our souls. Ultimately the question we come to ask God is "Lord, what do you want me to do?"

Our experience of God is always a mystery, never able to be fully understood or fully expressed. This is why meditating regularly is a vital dimension of our Christian prayer life. Meditation helps us own our faith. It helps us keep our focus and sense of direction as we journey in faith to God.

Contemplation

Of the three expressions of prayer, **contemplation** is the most challenging. At the same time it is the simple expression of the mystery of prayer. It unites us with the prayer of Christ.

The heart is the place of contemplative prayer. In contemplation we seek Jesus and, in him, the Father. It is "the prayer of the child of God" (CCC, 2712), "a *gift*, a grace" (CCC, 2713) and communion with the Holy Trinity, "a *gaze* of faith, fixed on Jesus" (CCC, 2715).

Through contemplative prayer we meet God in an experience that goes much deeper than meditation. We take whatever time is needed to allow God to reveal the secrets of our heart, to place ourselves in the deafening silence

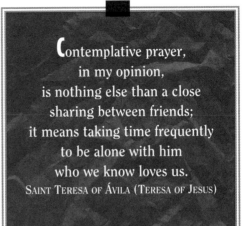

Contemplative prayer, in my opinion, is nothing else than a close sharing between friends; it means taking time frequently to be alone with him who we know loves us.
SAINT TERESA OF ÁVILA (TERESA OF JESUS)

of God. Contemplation is "the preeminently *intense time* of prayer. In it the Father strengthens our inner being with power through his Spirit 'that Christ may dwell in [our] hearts through faith' and we may be 'grounded in love'" (see Ephesians 3:16–17) (CCC, 2714).

Contemplative prayer is difficult because we are so easily prone to distraction. We are continuously tempted to look for things to do. We are so conditioned by our Western culture to fill what we perceive to be the silent "voids" of our lives. We forget God is present in those "voids," calling us to "spend time" with him.

This is precisely what contemplative prayer is about. It is about engaging deeply in the loving presence of God. Contemplation helps us quiet the noise of our lives in order to rest in the presence of God. There we see our most honest and true selves, and our love of God is tested in the fire of God's love for us. Therefore contemplation is not a place outside of us but rather a presence that we carry within us. The contemplative prayer is a prayer of the interior life of the Christian.

The Battle of Prayer

Prayer is at the heart of Christian life. It is not merely some mental activity, nor is it nothing more than an effort to reach a mental void. Prayer is more than words and postures, more than externals. It is the "living relationship of the children of God with their Father who is good beyond measure, with his Son Jesus Christ and with the Holy Spirit" (CCC, 2565).

Obstacles to Prayer

Prayer has repeatedly been described as a battle. It is a battle waged against ourselves and the powers in our culture that attempt to move us away from the love of God. It is a battle against the evil that we are faced with each day, evil that would otherwise consume us. In describing his life Paul wrote: "The willing is ready at hand, but doing the good is not" (Romans 7:18). We struggle with prayer in the same way for a variety of reasons.

Misguided Notions about Prayer.
Essential to understanding the profound mystery of prayer is that it is an invitation and a gift. Some Christians, however, see prayer more as an obligation. They see it as a task that is inconsistent with the rest of their lives. Prayer then becomes an interruption in our daily living.

Others live with the notion that prayer is completely up to them. They erroneously think that they are completely in control of the success and meaningfulness of prayer. They do not pray with the understanding that prayer is a response to the Spirit's invitation and inspiration. The "success" or "failure" of prayer flows from our willingness or refusal to surrender our minds and hearts to the Spirit. Genuine prayer emerges from the Holy Spirit and not merely from ourselves.

Mentality of the World. We live in a world in which science and reason prevail. Productivity and profit have become the proof of one's value. Comfort and sensuality dominate our efforts. A life of prayer stands in contradiction to these mind-sets. Yet, there is growing proof that more and more people are questioning these values and seeking a spirituality to refocus the direction of their lives. There is a real sense of the need for conversion as proclaimed in the Gospel.

Our response to God's love is the transforming activity that bonds us to God and to life itself. Prayer takes us deep within ourselves to meet God. But, through prayer, God drags us back to the world where we are to bring about the kingdom in love and compassion.

The Failure to Pray. Finally, we all face our own failure to pray. In everyone's life there are moments of ebb and flow during which we are more or less vigilant about our prayer. Often we become discouraged as we pray and see no results. We find ourselves in the desert of our faith—God seems to be absent, silent.

When this happens, when our pride is hurt, when our expectations are not met, when our selfishness (or sinfulness) gets the best of us, we are tempted to set prayer aside. To overcome these obstacles we need to gain humility, faith, trust, and perseverance. Meeting this "test" moves us to deeper prayer, to a more intimate relationship with the living God.

Distractions. Our lives are full of distractions that move us off the way of prayer. Yet, consciously and actively fighting these distractions and hunting them down—focusing on them—itself can become an even greater distraction. What we need to do when we are tempted by distractions to stop praying is to focus on what we are doing—opening our hearts to God. The Gospel tells us: "For where your treasure is, there also will your heart be" (Matthew 6:21).

Lack of Vigilance. We need to put our heart into prayer, and not fall into the trap of our distractions. We need to be ready to meet the Lord, and not worry about getting "oil, for our lamps." (See Matthew 25:1–13.)

Dryness. The desert is often used by spiritual writers to describe one of the major obstacles we face on our journey of prayer. The desert is a dry and lonely place. It describes the experience of feeling stranded. There is no oasis from which to be nourished. It is here that we face our limitations and our need for God. We come to realize that without God we are unable to make sense of our life. It is in the "desert" that we are most humbled as we come to deeply realize that we will not find meaning in the world of things, but in the mind and heart of God.

This is the place where people of prayer over the centuries have faced God in their nothingness, their poverty, their humility. It is the place where Jesus faced the temptations to abort his journey to his Father. It is here where the roots of our own faith grow deeper just as the roots of a tree grow deeper when it is dry. (See John 12:24.)

What the Documents Say

Throughout the history of the Church, men and women have committed themselves to living the religious life. In reflecting on the renewal of this way of life, the Church observed:

> In view of the hectic pace and tensions of modern life it is appropriate to give particular importance—over and above the daily rhythm of prayer—to those more prolonged moments of prayer, which can be variously spread out in different periods of the day.
>
> *Apostolic Exhortation on the Renewal of Religious Life*, 35

Discuss the ways that this teaching applies to the life of every Christian. Then brainstorm ways young people can make this teaching a part of their lives.

The Lack of Faith. We are pulled in many directions in our lives and we often lose our focus in our spiritual lives. The questions are: What do we treasure? What do we love? Where is our heart?

When we pray in times of need, distress, or suffering we turn to the Lord, asking, "Help me!" But do we really believe he will? Is our faith so trusting that we believe in Jesus' words, "[W]ithout me you can do nothing" (John 15:5)?

Acedia. Acedia is something like depression. We just cannot get up the energy to continue. There is little or no motivation to keep going. "The spirit is willing," Jesus pointed out, "but the flesh is weak" (Matthew 26:41). Laziness sets in.

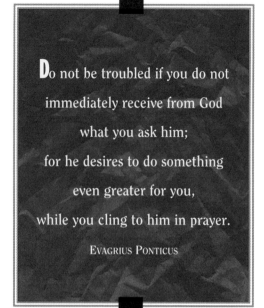

Do not be troubled if you do not immediately receive from God what you ask him; for he desires to do something even greater for you, while you cling to him in prayer.

EVAGRIUS PONTICUS

Trust and Perseverance

Our prayer life is built on trust and perseverance. When we feel that our prayer is not heard, our trust in God and our desire to continue in prayer can weaken. Such temptations call us to doubt Jesus, who revealed to us, "Your Father knows what you need before you ask him" (Matthew 6:8). When this happens, we continue on, trusting that "the Spirit too comes to the aid of our weakness" (Romans 8:26).

Filial Trust. Trusting God as his adopted children is what we are invited to do when we are in need. When the trials of life set in, at times when people might trust that God would aid them, many choose to stop praying, feeling that their prayers go unheard. At such moments, we need to trust God as Jesus asked.

Our first requests are not to be about what we are to wear or what we are

to eat. We first are to focus not on our need but on God, the Father who knows what we need before we ask. We bring our needs to God, trusting that our loving God—the God of Abraham, Isaac, and Moses, the Father of Jesus, our Savior—has always been and always will be faithful and merciful.

The prayer of trust is not so much about what we get out of praying as much as inviting and recognizing God's presence with us in our time of need. Relationships are not primarily about what we *get* but about what we *give*. Praying is ultimately about opening our heart to the presence of God filling our lives. This is the action of Salvation, of Redemption—the work of Jesus. We first pray, "your kingdom come." It is a prayer of surrender, "your will be done" (Matthew 6:10).

Persevering in Love. Praying always and in all ways, being aware of the presence of God in every moment, in the face of the stranger, in the presence of our enemies—this is the life of the prayerful person. The battle of prayer is ultimately one of trusting and persevering in love. This love opens our hearts to three enlightening and life-giving facts of faith about prayer:

. . . It Is Always Possible to Pray . . .

Saint John Chrysostom (c. 349–407) writes, "It is possible to offer fervent prayer even while walking in public or strolling alone, or seated in your shop . . . while buying or selling . . . while cooking." Put another way, there is no time that is not appropriate to pray. There is never a time when God is absent, so we are able to gather the attention of God at every moment of every day.

. . . Prayer Is Vital and Necessary . . .

The Christian life is nourished by the realization and the celebration of the presence of God in our midst. This can only be experienced in prayer, in the recognition of the covenant relationship of love that God has entered into with us.

Prayer and the Christian Life . . . . . . Are Inseparable . . . . . .

In order for us to live as children of God and followers of Jesus, we need to open ourselves to the presence of God with us. We are called to act with justice, to be light to a world darkened with sin and suffering. Standing up against the tide of popular opinion to defend the rights of the marginalized, oppressed, and the poor takes great strength. It takes courage that comes only from living our life with God.

Being a Christian is more than accepting a set of beliefs handed down to us. Being a Christian is about being a certain kind of human being. God calls us to be "holy as I am holy." We are called to be healers in a world of broken lives, broken hopes, and broken souls. Moral and ethical integrity doesn't happen by itself. It grows out of a life that is rooted in the soil of faith, nourished by love, cultivated with people of faith who share our journey. None of this is possible without a heart that is shaped in prayer.

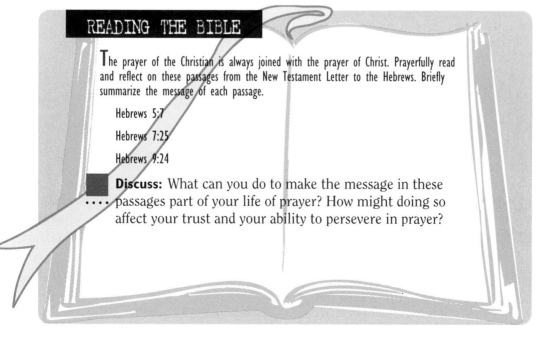

READING THE BIBLE

The prayer of the Christian is always joined with the prayer of Christ. Prayerfully read and reflect on these passages from the New Testament Letter to the Hebrews. Briefly summarize the message of each passage.

Hebrews 5:7

Hebrews 7:25

Hebrews 9:24

Discuss: What can you do to make the message in these passages part of your life of prayer? How might doing so affect your trust and your ability to persevere in prayer?

The Prayer of the Hour of Jesus

Jesus fulfilled the work of his Father in his Paschal mystery, his Death-Resurrection-Ascension.

On the night before he died, when his "hour" had come, Jesus prayed to the Father, "Father, the hour has come. Give glory to your son, so that your son may glorify you" (John 17:1).

Known as the "priestly" prayer of Jesus, it is the longest prayer of Jesus in the Gospels. It reveals to us the living relationship between Jesus and his Father, between Jesus and his followers, and between Jesus uniting his followers and the Father. It sums up the whole of God's loving plan of creation and salvation. His priestly prayer fulfills, from within, the petitions of the Lord's Prayer, which he taught us to pray.

Prayer

❖ ❖ ❖

Our Father, who art in heaven,

hallowed be thy name;

thy kingdom come,

thy will be done on earth
as it is in heaven.

Give us this day our daily bread,

and forgive us our trespasses,

as we forgive those who trespass
against us;

and lead us not into temptation,

but deliver us from evil.

Amen.

CHAPTER SUMMARY

Christian prayer is always prayer through Christ, with Christ, and in Christ, in the unity of the Holy Spirit. We express our prayer with trust and persevering love. In this chapter we learned:

1. We are invited by the Church to pray regularly, on a daily basis, through the Liturgy of the Hours, Sunday Eucharist, and in the seasonal feasts of the year.

2. Within the Christian tradition we have three basic expressions of prayer. They are vocal prayer, meditation, and contemplation. What they all have in common is a heart-centered attitude.

3. Vocal prayer is the prayer of the community. It is the heart seeking to be expressed in an outward fashion.

4. Meditation is a prayerful quest engaging thought, imagination, emotion, and desire to live our lives in Christ.

5. Contemplation is the simple expression of the mystery of prayer. A deep prayer, beyond meditation, contemplative prayer fixes us on the image of Jesus so that our lives might be purified in the presence of God.

6. If prayer is going to be meaningful and is to make a difference, then it will take dedication and work.

7. Prayer often grows dry and sometimes appears to be meaningless. These are the times when we ought to pray more fervently and trust in God.

EXPLORING OUR CATHOLIC FAITH

1. Listening to God's Word

John's Gospel records the "priestly" prayer of Jesus. Prayerfully read and reflect on John 17. Reflect on your own life and quietly pray this prayer to the Father.

2. Understanding the Teachings of the Catholic Church

Praying to Mary and with Mary has been the constant tradition of the Catholic Church. At the Second Vatican Council, the Church taught: "The entire body of the faithful pours forth urgent supplications to the Mother of God . . . that she, who aided the beginnings of the Church by her prayers, may now . . . intercede before her Son in the fellowship of all the saints until all families of people . . . may be happily gathered together in peace and harmony into one People of God" (*Dogmatic Constitution on the Church,* 69). What does this teaching tell us about the role of Mary in Christian prayer?

3. Reflecting on Our Catholic Faith

Reflect on this insight: "It is possible to offer fervent prayer even while walking in public or strolling alone, . . . while buying or selling" (Saint John Chrysostom). How does this insight help you lead a life of "constant" prayer? Write your thoughts in your journal.

4. Living Our Catholic Faith

Three specific expressions of prayer are vocal prayer, meditation, and contemplation. Choose one of these three expressions of prayers. Design and implement a plan to make it a part of your life each day.

CHAPTER 9

The Lord's Prayer

"This is how you are to pray:
Our Father in heaven . . ."

MATTHEW 6:9

What Do You Think?

In the space provided please explain why you agree or disagree with the statement "The Lord's Prayer is at the center of the Scriptures."

KEY TERMS

Apologist

catechumen

Didache

neophyte

In its "Points to Ponder" section, *Reader's Digest* carried this moving story by Cy Fey. An elderly man was weeping noticeably while standing alone at Washington's Vietnam Veterans' Memorial.

Moved by the sight, a young man walked over to the old man, put his hand on his shoulder, and said, "One of yours, sir?" The old man said softly, "Not *one* of them, son! *All* of them!"

This same spirit moved Jesus to pray not just for his disciples alone but for all believers.

From *Action 2000: Praying Scripture in a Contemporary Way* by Mark Link

Do my prayers reflect a concern for all people?

?

In the past chapters we have talked about various models, forms, and styles of prayer. We have explored the rich traditions and teachings of the Catholic Church as they have been presented in the *Catechism of the Catholic Church*. We have also discussed the nature and importance of prayer not only as our communication with the Creator God but also as the living relationship of the children of God, Father, Son, and Holy Spirit. In this chapter we will look at the Lord's Prayer through the lens of the Catechism. Here we will discover the rich beauty that is contained in the prayer and more fully realize the important place that it holds in the Christian journey.

(*Catechism of the Catholic Church*, 2759–2760)

Prayer of Jesus

We have just begun to scratch the surface of our spirituality. Our world takes on a whole different look when we recognize that it is colored with the sacred. We have embarked on a journey, a journey within *and* without. We have begun to walk the path of Christian prayer, a path that presents new choices for us each day. Our spiritual lives continue to grow because we have made deliberate decisions to accept the message of Jesus, to live as he has modeled life for us.

The most important reality about prayer is the fact that it is God whom we are invited to address as "Abba," loving Father, who initiates this relationship of intimacy with us. "As proof that you are children, God sent the spirit of his Son into our hearts, crying out, 'Abba, Father!' " (Galatians 4:6). It is God, through the workings of the Holy Spirit, that lives within the depths of our hearts.

Our success at prayer relies on our willingness to surrender our lives, desires, will, hopes, dreams, and life vision to God. The Israelites were constantly challenged by the prophets to surrender their hearts to God and to trust that he, who was always faithful to them even in their infidelity, would care for them. After we have given our hearts over to God we begin to realize that our lives are transformed, little by little, over a period of time by love. In the quiet of the moment, we are able to focus on the burning love of God. We are able to surrender ourselves to the fire of the Father's love as Jesus did in prayer. "[N]ot as I will," he prayed in the Garden of Gethsemani, "but as you will" (Matthew 26:39). As Jesus prayed, he taught us to pray.

Jesus Teaches Us to Pray

"Lord, teach us to pray just as John taught his disciples" (Luke 11:1), one of his disciples asked Jesus. In response, Jesus taught his followers the prayer that we know as the Lord's Prayer, or the Our Father.

One can imagine how the disciples must have gazed on Jesus all the times he prayed. There must have been something genuinely different about his posture, more his attitude rather than physical posture, when he approached his Father in this intimate form of communication.

Jesus prayed. He prayed in the Temple. He prayed in the synagogue. Jesus

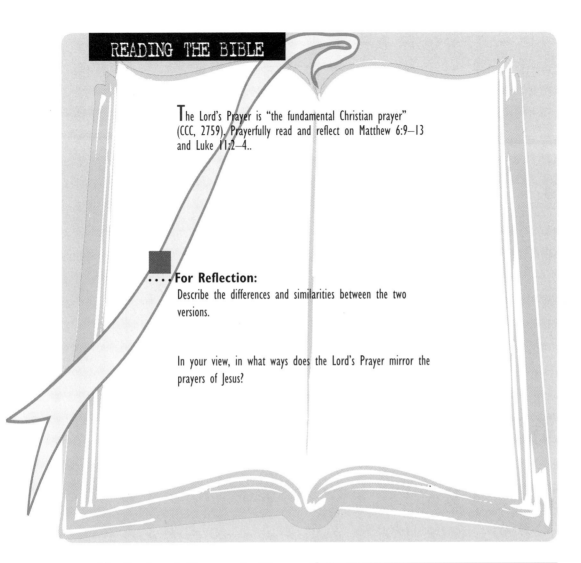

The Lord's Prayer is "the fundamental Christian prayer" (CCC, 2759). Prayerfully read and reflect on Matthew 6:9–13 and Luke 11:2–4..

For Reflection:

Describe the differences and similarities between the two versions.

In your view, in what ways does the Lord's Prayer mirror the prayers of Jesus?

prayed in the desert. He prayed with his disciples and alone.

But in this instance his disciples approached him and asked him to teach them to pray. He responded by inviting them to pray with the same level of intimacy and trust as he did.

Saint Luke gives a brief accounting of five petitions (Luke 11:2–4) while Saint Matthew gives a more developed version of seven petitions (Matthew 6:9–13). It is Matthew's version that has become part of the living prayer tradition of the Church.

(CCC, 2761–2766)

The Fundamental Christian Prayer

The Christian writer and **Apologist** Tertullian (c. 160–c. 225) taught that the Lord's Prayer is the "summary of the whole gospel" *(On Prayer)*. The Lord's Prayer expresses the desire of our hearts to seek God above all things, to share in the love of God, and to surrender in trust to God's mercy. The prayer places our fundamental needs at the feet of God in honor and trust.

"[S]ince everyone has petitions which are peculiar to his circumstances," Tertullian writes, "the regular and appropriate prayer [the Lord's Prayer] is said first, as the foundation of further desires" *(On Prayer)*. This was the prayer central to the early Christian Church and continues to be the focal prayer of the Christian Church everywhere.

The ancient prayer of the Lord's Prayer is one that rests in the center of Christian spirituality. It reflects the deep longings that human beings have for truth, love, and wholeness, and it recognizes that we are ultimately reliant on God for genuine happiness. The prayer affirms the intimacy experienced between the Israelites and God and draws all people to that same closeness.

At the Center of Sacred Scripture

Run through all the words of the holy prayers [in Scripture], and I do not think that you will find anything in them that is not contained and included in the Lord's Prayer.

SAINT AUGUSTINE

In the Gospel of Luke the Christian faith that all the Scriptures are fulfilled in Christ is clearly passed on to us (see Luke 24:44). The Law, the Prophets, and the psalms find their completeness and fullness in Christ. This is the "Good News" of the Gospel.

The human struggle for identity, hope, wholeness, and purpose has been finally addressed. We find the answer to our deepest questions in Jesus. Saint Matthew summarizes this in the Sermon on the Mount (see Matthew 5–7). The Lord's Prayer is a summary of the Gospel proclamation.

The Sermon on the Mount and the Lord's Prayer are foundational for Christian living. The Sermon on the Mount expresses the basic values and attitudes that give shape to our actions. The Lord's Prayer expresses our deepest desires for God and the inner movements of our heart. Both the teachings of the Sermon on the Mount and the prayer, which is at its center, are a summary of our life in Christ. "The rightness of our life in [Jesus] will depend on the rightness of our prayer" (CCC, 2764).

The Lord's Prayer

The title of this prayer comes from the Latin *"oratio Dominica,"* meaning that this is the prayer that has been given to us by God through his Son our Lord Jesus.

. . . . The Prayer of the Lord . . . .

Jesus is the master and model of our prayer. In him we find *the prayer* that emerges from the roots of human life—from our dependence on and trust in God. Jesus is the very Word of God made flesh. Jesus reveals to us what our relationship with God truly is.

Jesus prays from the depth of his own human heart, a heart compassionate with the human struggle to find meaning. His prayer to the Father originates in his human heart, which he shares with all humanity. His prayer becomes our prayer.

. . . . A Prayer of Our Heart . . . .

The Spirit teaches us how to pray every vocal prayer as a prayer of our heart. Through the invitation to prayer the Spirit ignites a spark within our hearts, a spark that illuminates the presence of God within us, and beyond us. He draws us closer and deeper into the presence of God, moving us to address God as Jesus did, *"Abba, Father"* (Mark 14:36).

The Lord's Prayer not only expresses our need for God but also reveals the relationship that God invites us to. It is the Spirit of God in our hearts who urges us to pray with trust to the Father (see Galatians 4:6). Praying the Our Father is truly an expression of our life of communion with the Holy Trinity.

For Reflection

Saint Thomas Aquinas (c. 1225–1274), a Doctor of the Church and a follower of Saint Dominic, was one of the great teachers of the Church. He was known as a scholar and preacher whose life was nourished by Scripture and contemplative prayer. He wrote this about the Lord's Prayer:

> The Lord's Prayer is the most perfect of prayers. . . . In it we ask, not only for all the things we can rightly desire, but also in the sequence that they should be desired. This prayer not only teaches us to ask for things, but in what order we should desire them.
>
> SAINT THOMAS AQUINAS

. . . . Discuss:

What does Thomas mean when he says the Lord's Prayer teaches us the "order" we should "desire" things?

(CCC, 2767–2772)

The Prayer of the Church

The praying of the Lord's Prayer unites all Christians. Saint John Chrysostom wrote that the Lord's Prayer is the common ground for all Christians. "For he did not say 'my Father' who art in heaven, but 'our' Father, offering petitions from the common body" *(Homily in Matthew)*. It is the basis of prayer for all Christians. It has been a source of spiritual nurture and strength from the beginning of the Church.

Apostolic Tradition

The first and earliest Christian believers were Jews who became followers of the way of Jesus. They naturally drew from the richness of their religious beliefs and practices. Among these was praying what was called the "Eighteen Benedictions" each day. We read in the **Didache** that the early believers, who were Jewish, replaced these benedictions with the practice of praying the Lord's Prayer three times a day.

Liturgical Prayer

The Lord's Prayer, from the earliest days of the Church, has been rooted in liturgical prayer. In all liturgical settings the Lord's Prayer is a central focus in the common prayer of the assembly. In the three Sacraments of Christian Initiation—Baptism, Confirmation, and the Eucharist— we recognize the communal character of this prayer.

Baptism and Confirmation. In Baptism and Confirmation we see how the Lord's Prayer reflects the reality of new birth into the life of Christ. This is why the writings of the early Church fathers about the Our Father are addressed to the **catechumens**—those studying and considering becoming members of the Church—and to the **neophytes**— the newly initiated members of the Christian community.

Eucharist. In the Sacrament of the Eucharist, the Lord's Prayer unites the whole Church. There we find the full meaning of the prayer. It unites the Eucharistic Prayer and the Communion Rite. On one hand it gathers and sums up the petitions and the intercessions expressed in the Eucharistic Prayer; on the other, it opens the door to the Kingdom of God, the eternal union with the loving God.

The Lord's Prayer expresses our faith that life has its beginning and end in God. When prayed in the context of the Eucharist, the Lord's Prayer reminds us that the time of Salvation that began with the outpouring of the Holy Spirit will be fulfilled with the Lord's return. From this faith, hope, and love, we pray seven petitions of the Lord's Prayer that address our deepest hungers and needs. We yearn for oneness with God, our Creator. We hope that we will one day fully become what we have been created to be. When we participate in the Eucharist and pray the Lord's Prayer, we look eagerly for the Lord's return, "until he comes."

Prayer

❖ ❖ ❖

At Mass we pray:

> Our Father, who art in heaven,
>   hallowed be thy name;
>
> thy kingdom come,
>
> thy will be done on earth as it is
>   in heaven.
>
> Give us this day our daily bread,
>
> and forgive us our trespasses,
>   as we forgive those who
>   trespass against us;
>
> and lead us not into temptation,
>
> but deliver us from evil.

The priest continues:

> Deliver us, Lord, we pray, from
> every evil, graciously grant peace
> in our days, that, by the help of
> your mercy, we may be always
> free from sin and safe from all
> distress as we await the blessed
> hope and the coming of our
> Savior, Jesus Christ.

The assembly concludes:

> For the kingdom, the power
>   and the glory are yours
>   now and for ever.

> The Order of Mass
> *Roman Missal*

REVIEW

IMPORTANT TERMS TO KNOW

Apologist—a Christian writer who wrote between A.D. 100 and A.D. 300, defending the faith against pagan accusations and persecutions

catechumen—an unbaptized person participating in the preparation process of the initiation into the Church

Didache—the earliest gathering of materials and documents used to teach the faith of the Christians

neophyte—a newly initiated member of the Church

CHAPTER SUMMARY

The Lord's Prayer is the model prayer. Praying the prayer that Jesus taught us helps us grow in our relationship with God. In this chapter we learned:

1. The disciples asked Jesus to teach them to pray. The response to this request was Jesus teaching them the Our Father, which has become the cornerstone of Christian prayer.

2. The Lord's Prayer is at the center of the Scriptures and it summarizes the entire Gospel.

3. It is called the Lord's Prayer because it comes from the mind of God and the heart of Jesus. Jesus is our master and model of living and praying.

4. The Lord's Prayer is the ultimate and all-consuming prayer of the Christian Church. Integrated into the prayer is an eschatological character, that is, it reminds us of and embraces the belief that there will be an end, and for those who believe, the journey will lead to full life with God.

EXPLORING OUR CATHOLIC FAITH

1. Listening to God's Word

Read the shorter version of the Our Father as found in Luke 11:2–4. What is missing in this wording that is found in the traditional words that you know? What difference does this make?

2. Understanding the Teachings of the Catholic Church

In the Lord's Prayer we have an intimate relationship with God, which God initiates with us. Truly we can call God "Our Father." Reflect in your journal on what

this close personal relationship with God means in your life.

3. Reflecting on Our Catholic Faith

Discuss the entire Gospel message and how these ideas are summarized in the Our Father.

4. Living Our Catholic Faith

In the early Church, Christians prayed the Lord's Prayer three times a day. Pray the Lord's Prayer at three different times today. Say the words slowly and think about their meaning.

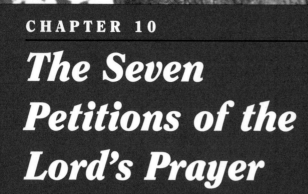

CHAPTER 10

The Seven Petitions of the Lord's Prayer

God sent the spirit of his Son into our hearts, crying out, "Abba, Father!"

GALATIANS 4:6

In the space provided write "A" if you agree with the statement, "D" if you disagree with it, or "N" if you have no opinion about it.

_____ 1. The Lord's Prayer was given to the Apostles by John the Baptist.

_____ 2. Most people who pray the Lord's Prayer don't really understand it.

_____ 3. The Lord's Prayer is the prayer that is at the center of Christian spirituality.

_____ 4. Prayer cannot be limited to written prayers that I learned as a child.

_____ 5. The Lord's Prayer is an old prayer that should be updated.

Where are you going to college? What will be your major?" Kim kept complaining. "I wish people would just stop asking!"

"I agree, Kim," Daniel responded in sympathy. "If people would only just stop asking and asking and asking."

"It seems like all my life people have been asking me what I want to do," Kim went on. "When I was little, I was going to be an astronaut. Then I thought being a social worker like my dad would be a great job. There are so many choices. I just don't know. I was hoping that going to college would help me sort it out."

Do you get tired of people asking you the same questions over and over? Why is that?

Praying is one way we help discern what God wants us to do and how we can use the gifts God has blessed us with. Do you think God gets tired of us asking him the same questions over and over? Why or why not?

KEY TERMS

Divine Providence

Heaven

holy

Kingdom of God

petition

temptation

There was a song some years ago sung by Bette Midler that talked about coming to see God "from a distance," somewhere beyond us, watching us, somewhat disinterested in our lives, yet connecting in some fashion to our human experience. There is some truth to the song at one level—God is *beyond* us. But in both the Old and the New Testaments God reveals himself equally to be the living God who dwells in our midst. His name is Yahweh, Emmanuel, "God-with-us."

We who believe in Jesus believe that this truth about God is more fully revealed in Jesus, the Word of God became flesh (see John 1:1–14).

It is with this faith that we are able to utter those words that Jesus taught us, "Our Father . . ." For the followers of Jesus this prayer becomes a communion that unites people with God and with each other, celebrating an entirely unique and fresh spirituality. In this chapter we will uncover and discover the profound spirituality that is revealed in this prayer.

(*Catechism of the Catholic Church*, 2777–2796)

Our Father

Rooted in the Israelite faith in God, Christianity is a religion lived and realized in community.

We Dare to Say Father!

This faith is expressed at the very beginning of the Lord's Prayer. We weave ourselves together as a community in our embrace of the wondrous God. We call on God as "ours."

In a society that covets the notion of individualism, the Our Father breaks all social conventions. The prayer doesn't begin "my" Father. This prayer states that we are in communion with the Christian community, sharing together in the presence of God. We lay claim to God as *our* God. We acknowledge that it is God for whom we are accountable and who is accountable to us as our Parent, our Creator.

For the Israelites, God revealed himself as both immanent and transcendent, both dwelling with them and acting on their behalf and yet beyond. The Israelites believed that they belonged to God, and that God belonged to them. Theirs was a relationship of awe and wonder, of deep love and mutuality.

Jesus revealed the deep mystery of God that the Israelites first came to know. Jesus spoke to God with the bold familiarity of a child to a loving father. He taught us to address our God in the same way.

The Lord's Prayer frames our relationship with God. God is our "Abba," our loving Father, the source of our life.

Ever since the early Church, the Christian assembly has been invited to pray to God the Father in Heaven with boldness and trust: We dare to say, Our Father. "We can invoke God as 'Father' because *he is revealed to us* by his Son become man and because his Spirit makes him known to us" (CCC, 2780).

Since we call and pray to God as Father, we express our faith that we live in communion with God. We have been freely adopted by God. We are adopted children of God, through his only Son, Jesus. We adore God the Father for now we are reborn to new life.

This adoption requires two things on our part: continual conversion and new life. Saint John Chrysostom puts it this way: "You cannot call the God of all kindness your Father if you preserve a cruel and inhuman heart; for in this case you no longer have in you the marks of the heavenly Father's kindness" *(On the Our Father)*.

For Reflection

The Our Father is the fundamental Christian prayer. List the celebrations in which you have prayed this prayer with others.

When have you prayed this prayer alone? Why did you choose to pray it?

Who Art in Heaven . . .

For many, what first comes to mind when they hear the word **Heaven** is a distant place where God and the angels and the Saints live. But this is not what the writers meant when they spoke of Heaven. Rather, they used the word and concept *Heaven* to first of all convey their faith in the majesty of God. God was the almighty one, the Creator, greater than any creature and all creatures combined.

> From heaven the LORD looks down and observes the whole human race,
> Surveying from the royal throne all who dwell on earth.
> The one who fashioned the hearts of them all knows all their works.
> **Psalm 33:13–15**

Second, the faith term *Heaven* passed on to us the truth that our life with God is a way of being, a living relationship. This relationship is described as a "covenant" freely entered into with us by God. The story of this Covenant as told by Scripture is one of the fidelity and loyalty of God and the all-too-often disloyalty of his people. Restored in Christ, the New Covenant, we are reconciled with God and look forward in hope to living a life of eternal happiness with God. We look forward to Heaven.

Jesus often taught about the Kingdom of Heaven, using parables (see Matthew 13). Paul too encourages his readers to live their lives focused on "Heaven."

It is from this faith and hope we pray "Our Father who art in heaven."

READING THE BIBLE

Prayerfully read this Gospel passage.

If then you were raised with Christ, seek what is above, where Christ is seated at the right hand of God. Think of what is above, not of what is on earth. For you have died, and your life is hidden with Christ in God. When Christ your life appears, then you too will appear with him in glory.

Colossians 3:1–4

What is your image of Heaven?

What do you hope it will be like?

The First Three Petitions

Prayer places us in the presence of our God. With open hands we enter into the Lord's Prayer and call upon God as our Father. We locate God in a place beyond us, Heaven. In the Lord's Prayer we offer our very lives to God and identify areas of our day-to-day life that we wish to give over to God, who heals the brokenness of our soul. When we say "Our Father who art in heaven," we surrender ourselves to the Spirit. It is the Spirit of God who "stirs up in our hearts seven petitions, seven blessings" (CCC, 2803).

The Our Father contains seven **petitions** which reflect who God is, who we are as creatures and children of the Father. The first three petitions focus on the "majesty" of God "in heaven": "Hallowed be thy name," "Thy kingdom come," "Thy will be done on earth as it is in heaven." In none of these three petitions do we directly mention ourselves.

When we say "Our Father who art in heaven," we surrender ourselves to the Spirit. Led by the Spirit, however, praying these petitions helps us focus on our lives. We focus on God, who dwells within us, as the center of our lives. Praying these first three petitions helps us transform our lives into living prayers of blessing and adoration, praise, and thanksgiving to God, who is the source of our life and every blessing.

The first three petitions draw us closer to God. *Thy* name, *thy* kingdom, *thy* will—these are the words of a humble

For Reflection

. . . .

God reveals to us that we are to be holy because he is holy. In what sense do you consider yourself to be holy?

What do you need to do to make your life more holy?

Discuss: Praising, adoring, and blessing God as "holy" includes both our *life* and our *prayer*.

heart. We don't mention ourselves. We aren't at the center of the universe— God is. In the first three petitions we focus on God as the center of our lives rather than ourselves. The last four affirm our dependence on God and surrender to God our weakness.

Hallowed Be Thy Name . . .

Since I, the LORD,
brought you up from the land
of Egypt
that I might be your God,
you shall be holy,
because I am holy.

Leviticus 11:45

The Israelite people believed not only in the holiness of God but in their own holiness. This belief was at the heart of the Covenant, of their relationship with God.

In the story of creation and the history of God's dealing with the people, we are constantly reminded of the holiness of God and our call to be **holy.** Created in the image and likeness of God, we share in the holiness of God.

In his priestly prayer Jesus addresses his Father as holy and prays, "Holy Father, keep them in your name that you have given me, so that they may be one just as we are" (John 17:11).

When we pray the Lord's Prayer we affirm and acknowledge the holiness of God, which is the root of the mystery of God and God's loving plan of creation and Salvation for us. In so doing we bless and adore God. We praise God and thank God for sharing with us his life and love, his mercy and forgiveness. We call ourselves to conversion—to be holy because God is holy, to be holy because we have been created to live in communion with him.

For Reflection

What can you do to make your world one that is more just, more loving, and more in harmony with the vision of Jesus?

How can you be a part in the building of the kingdom?

Thy Kingdom Come...

The announcement and proclamation of the **Kingdom of God** is at the heart of the Gospel message. John the Baptist announces Jesus and his work, saying, "Repent, for the kingdom of heaven is at hand!" (Matthew 3:2). And in describing the work of Jesus, the Gospel of Matthew tells us, "Jesus went around to all the towns and villages, teaching in their synagogues, proclaiming the gospel of the kingdom" (Matthew 9:35).

Initiated in the Paschal Mystery of Christ—in his Death and Resurrection, the kingdom preached and established by Jesus will fully come about when Christ comes again in glory. In praying this petition of the Lord's Prayer, we adore God as our Creator and Savior. We bless, praise, and thank God for the plan of his creation and Salvation. We pray that his will be realized and his kingdom (or reign) come to be.

READING THE BIBLE

Jesus often preached about the Kingdom of God. Prayerfully read and reflect on these parables, which Jesus used to preach about the kingdom. Briefly describe in your own words what they tell us about the kingdom.

Matthew 13:24–30 (parable of Weeds among the Wheat)

Matthew 13:31–32 (parable of the Mustard Seed)

Matthew 25:31–46 (The Judgment of the Nations)

At the same time we are committing ourselves to work toward the coming of that Kingdom of God on Earth through dedicating our lives to the will of God.

> For the grace of God has appeared, saving all and training us to reject godless ways and worldly desires and to live temperately, justly, and devoutly in this age, as we await the blessed hope, the appearance of the glory of the great God and of our savior Jesus Christ.
>
> **Titus 2:11–13**

Thy Will Be Done on Earth as It Is in Heaven . . .

In the New Testament Letter to Timothy we read that God "wills everyone to be saved and to come to knowledge of the truth" (1 Timothy 2:4). This third petition of the Lord's Prayer expresses our deepest desire to live the Great Commandment. We pray that the will of God be realized—in our own lives and in the lives of others. It is our expression of unconditional, selfless love that the Kingdom of God be realized in every moment of our lives.

We struggle to find the will of God for us. We each have our own wills to contend with and may often confuse God's will with our own. Discerning God's will is the work of our cooperating with the Holy Spirit.

Jesus' ministry and work was about fulfilling God's plan of Salvation and Redemption—doing the will of God. His will became God's will. The Gospel reminds us that Jesus prayed, "Father, if you are willing, take this cup away from me; still, not my will but yours be done"

(Luke 22:42). Through the power of prayer and through the help of the Holy Spirit we too can discern the will of God for us and receive the courage to do it.

Give Us This Day Our Daily Bread . . .

This petition is an expression of trust in **Divine Providence.** We believe and trust that we are loved by God and that he has pledged to care for us. We place our needs—both material and spiritual—before him.

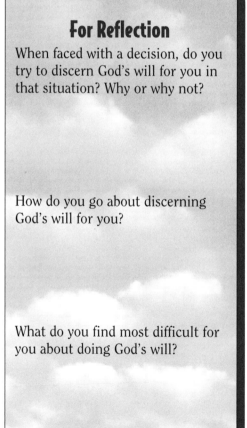

For Reflection

When faced with a decision, do you try to discern God's will for you in that situation? Why or why not?

How do you go about discerning God's will for you?

What do you find most difficult for you about doing God's will?

Give us . . . Jesus revealed the quality of this trusting confidence. "Amen, I say to you, unless you turn and become like children, you will not enter the kingdom of heaven" (Matthew 18:3). Jesus uses this image of children to reveal our relationship with God. Children naturally and rightfully trust that their parents will always protect, nourish, nurture, and love them—they believe that they always want what is good for them.

The nature of this bond between God and his people is what this petition is based on. We ask God for what we need to sustain our lives and we trust that God will provide. This petition "glorifies our Father by acknowledging how good he is, beyond all goodness" (CCC, 2828). In the sense that we trust that God "gives us" what we need (more than what we want) reflects that unconditional nature of our trust in the covenant God made with us in Christ.

The petition always expresses our desire to live the *entire* Great Commandment. We pray not only for ourselves but for all those who are in need. We are a faith community who believes not only that God is a loving and generous God but that we are to act lovingly and generously to all without exception. In praying this petition, we call upon God to show his love and care not only for us but also for others. Jesus commanded us to "love one another. As I have loved you, so you also should love one another" (John 13:34). When we pray this petition, we commit ourselves to being instruments of that action.

Our daily bread . . . What is this bread we pray for? " 'Our' bread is the 'one' loaf for the 'many.' In the Beatitudes 'poverty' is the virtue of sharing: it calls us to communicate and share both

For Reflection

What would you say are among your greatest needs?

What is *your* daily bread?

Does it make sense that we need to be "bread" for others?

material and spiritual goods, not by coercion but out of love, so that the abundance of some may remedy the needs of others" (CCC, 2833).

The image "bread" points to both the bread that sustains our body and to the bread that sustains our soul. In Jesus' reply to the temptation of the devil, he quotes Deuteronomy 8:3:

"One does not live by bread alone,
but by every word that comes forth
from the mouth of God."
Matthew 4:4

Just as there is hunger and need for bread to feed the body, so too is there hunger and need for the presence of God in our hearts and in the world. In this petition the Spirit moves us to pray for all these needs. Several years ago Blessed Mother Teresa of Calcutta, while visiting the United States, observed that the greatest poverty she saw was our spiritual poverty. Through this petition of the Our Father we ask God, above all, to reach into our hearts and reshape us and to fill those spiritual hungers.

For Reflection

What would you say are among your greatest needs?

What is the "daily bread" you are most in need of?

Discuss: How will filling that need help you?

And Forgive Us Our Trespasses, as We Forgive Those Who Trespass Against Us . . .

The Great Commandment is indivisible.

> ■ . . . If anyone says, "I love God," but hates his brother, he is a liar; for whoever does not love a brother whom he has seen cannot love God whom he has not seen. This is the commandment we have from him: whoever loves God must also love his brother.
> **I John 4:20–21**

This love includes forgiving "seventy-seven" times—or forgiving "always."

Forgive us our trespasses . . . Like the prodigal son (Luke 15:11–32) and the tax collector (Luke 18:33), we recognize that we sin. We recognize and admit that in our wrongfully perceived self-interest, we turn away from God. When we come to that realization and "self-accusation," we reach out to God, trusting that he is "always" willing to forgive us.

The truth is that not all the decisions we make are good decisions. We hurt others and we are hurt by others. Look around. See the amount of pain that we cause one another. The daily newspaper, the twenty-four hour news channel records these choices and their harmful effects. It is a matter of public record.

And so we petition "Forgive us our trespasses, as . . ." Forgive us—but only "as" we forgive others. We accept Jesus' clarification and take him at his Word: "If you forgive others their transgressions, your heavenly Father will forgive you. But if you do not forgive others, neither will your Father forgive your transgressions" (Matthew 6:14–15).

As we forgive those who trespass against us . . . We earlier reflected on the reality that we are called to be holy as God is holy. A dimension of that call is the foundation of this petition: we are to forgive as God forgives. Only the Spirit can help us "be kind to one another, compassionate, forgiving one another as God has forgiven you in Christ" (Ephesians 4:32).

In this petition we pray, "God, please forgive me for the times that I have sinned against others because of the harm I have done, but, Lord, only forgive me to the extent that I am willing to forgive those who have harmed me"—a commitment and request that applies even to forgiving our enemies—and to those who cause us great harm! Forgive me but no more and no less than I am willing to forgive others.

In this posture and attitude of prayer, we image and take part in Christ's own attitude lived out in his Paschal Mystery—the mystery of his Death-Resurrection-Ascension. We surrender ourselves to such forgiveness, trusting and believing it is the true path to new life and to glory.

READING THE BIBLE

Jesus continuously calls us to forgive as God forgives. Prayerfully read and reflect on Matthew 18:23–35, the parable of the Merciless Servant.

Why is the servant "merciless"?

Discuss:

How does the parable of the Merciless Servant help us understand the meaning of the words we pray in the Lord's Prayer?

When it seems impossible, we turn to God, believing in Jesus and his Word, "for God all things are possible" (Matthew 19:26).

And Lead Us Not into Temptation . . .

We are all faced with difficult choices in our lives. Some choices look really good on the outset, but after closer scrutiny they are really not what they appear to be. In this petition we acknowledge the struggle between good and evil that goes on not only in the world around us but also in the depth of our hearts.

A common image used to portray **temptation** is that of the cartoon character who, when faced with the decision whether to cook the mouse for supper, is confronted with an angel and a devil. The angel pleads for the life of the victim, while the devil prods him to throw the mouse into the frying pan and have it for dinner. There is a comical yet profound truth to this image as it seems to mirror our experience of temptation.

We believe that it is not God who tempts us. God wants to set us free from evil and sin. In this petition we are asking that God help us not to "yield to temptation"

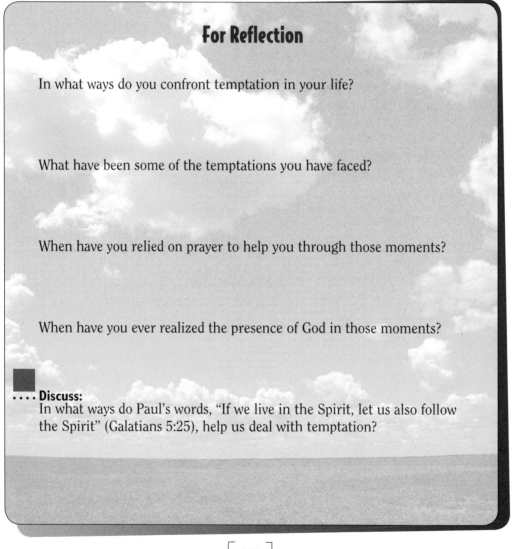

For Reflection

In what ways do you confront temptation in your life?

What have been some of the temptations you have faced?

When have you relied on prayer to help you through those moments?

When have you ever realized the presence of God in those moments?

Discuss:
In what ways do Paul's words, "If we live in the Spirit, let us also follow the Spirit" (Galatians 5:25), help us deal with temptation?

and make such wrong, or evil, choices that tempt us, or present themselves to us as "good." When faced with such temptations, we trust that what Paul wrote to the Christians living in Corinth also applies to us:

> God is faithful and will not let you be tried beyond your strength; but with the trial he will also provide a way out, so that you may be able to bear it.
> **1 Corinthians 10:13**

It is only through prayer and the help of the Holy Spirit that we gain the wisdom and courage, perseverance and strength to "unmask" the deception that presents evil as good. This petition "implores the Spirit of discernment and strength" (CCC, 2863). This ability to stand against those moments in our lives where we are faced with temptation is only possible through prayer. For through all of the temptation that we face, God is present, desiring that we would choose the path that unites us more closely to him.

But Deliver Us from Evil . . .

In this final petition we ask that God protect us from all that is evil and contrary to the heart of God. In this petition evil is not an abstraction, but a person, Satan, who opposes God (see CCC, 2851) and who is the tempter, the evil one. In the Gospel of John we read, "I do not ask that you take them out of the world but that you keep them from the evil one" (John 17:15).

Our culture, our society, our world is permeated ever so subtly by the effects and influence of evil—present and past. We are confronted with them every day. We are called to stand against evil in every form—in whatever form it expresses itself.

When we ask to be delivered from the evil one, we pray to be freed from all evils—past, present, *and* future.

We ask that God give us the courage and the strength to face evil and to help create the kingdom, trusting and believing that the Paschal Mystery of Jesus' Death and Resurrection has claimed victory over all evil forever!

(CCC, 2855–2856)

The Final Doxology

This final ending to the Lord's Prayer echoes the first three petitions to the prayer—the glory of God, the coming of the Reign of God, and the power of the love of God.

For the Kingdom, the Power and the Glory Are Yours Now and For Ever . . .

In this brief hymn of adoration and praise, we conclude as we began. We acknowledge in wonder and awe the awesomeness of God. It is God who is the giver of all life and all goodness. There is no beginning or end to God's love, God's beauty, God's care for us. We adore and give thanks to God the Father, God the Redeemer, God the Sanctifier.

Amen!

Finally we end this prayer with confidence and faith. We acclaim, "Amen," "So be it," or "Yes, God!" It is a way in which we give thanks and honor to God and express our total dependence on God our Creator. In God we find the strength to live and the courage to take up our cross and love.

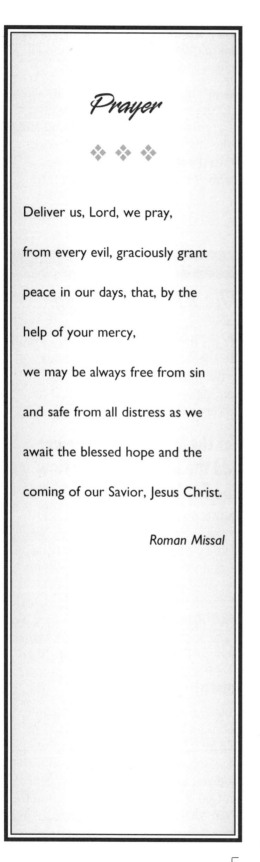

Prayer

❖ ❖ ❖

Deliver us, Lord, we pray,

from every evil, graciously grant

peace in our days, that, by the

help of your mercy,

we may be always free from sin

and safe from all distress as we

await the blessed hope and the

coming of our Savior, Jesus Christ.

Roman Missal

REVIEW

IMPORTANT TERMS TO KNOW

Divine Providence—God's loving and faithful caring for us and guiding us

Heaven—eternal happiness and life with God and the Communion of Saints for all eternity. It is the state of supreme, definitive happiness that human hearts deeply desire.

holy—a word derived from the Hebrew, meaning "to be apart from or separate from"; to set apart from for religious purposes; it is unique to God and only to God.

Kingdom of God—image or symbol used in Scripture that describes the living of all people and creation in communion with God. The kingdom will come about when Christ comes again in glory.

petition—an earnest request; a sincere desire for something

temptation—the desire or attraction to choose to do or say something wrong or not to do what we know we have the responsibility to do

CHAPTER SUMMARY

When we pray the Our Father we express an entirely new relationship with God. In praying the Lord's Prayer we are journeying back to the heart of God, to our homeland to which we already belong. In this chapter we learned:

1. There are seven petitions in the Lord's Prayer. The first three glorify God. The last four recognize our dependence on God.

2. The first three petitions strengthen us in faith, hope, and charity.

3. The first petition recognizes the intimate relationship we have with our God as Father.

4. In the second petition we look to the return of Christ.

5. In the third petition we ask that his will

and ours be united with Jesus.

6. The fourth petition expresses our dependence on God for our material needs as well as our spiritual needs.

7. The fifth petition begs for the mercy of God for the harm that we have done.

8. We ask in the sixth petition that God would keep us from temptation not to do God's will.

9. In the seventh petition we ask that God will deliver us from all that is evil, most especially from the Evil One, who is Satan.

10. *Amen* is a word that means "So be it."

EXPLORING OUR CATHOLIC FAITH

1. Listening to God's Word

"[I]f one is devout and does his will, [God] listens to him" (John 9:31). Prayer is a very powerful instrument in our lives. Discuss examples of the power of prayer in your life and in the lives of others.

2. Understanding the Teachings of the Catholic Church

One of the early Church fathers, Origen, said this about temptation: "God does not want to impose the good, but wants free beings. . . . [T]emptation reveals it in order to teach us to know ourselves, and in this way we discover our evil inclinations and are obliged to give thanks for the good that temptation has revealed to us"

(Origen, De orat. 29: PG 11, 544CD. as quoted in CCC, 2284).

3. Reflecting on Our Catholic Faith

Saint Cyril of Jerusalem says, " 'Heaven' could also be those who bear the image of the heavenly world, and in whom God dwells and tarries" (CCC, 2794). Think about this quote and write in your journal how you can be an image of Heaven.

4. Living Our Catholic Faith

In this chapter you studied each individual petition of the Lord's Prayer. Spend some time in praying the Lord's Prayer very slowly, thinking and meditating on each petition and part of the prayer.

Index

A

"Abba, Father," 31, 102, 106, 112–13. *see also* God the Father
Abraham, prayer of faith of, 21
acedia, 96, 98
adoration, prayer of, 45
    definition of, 52
advice, seeking, 78
Ambrose (Saint), 27
Amen, meaning of, 123
Annunciation, 36
apologist, 103, 108
Apostles, 42–43
apostolic tradition, Lord's Prayer in, 107
art, 69

B

Baptism, Lord's prayer in, 107
Blessed Sacrament, 83, 84
blessing, prayer of, 44
    definition of, 52
bread, daily, 119–20

C

candles, 68
catechist(s), 81
catechumen(s), 107, 108
centering prayer, 32
charity (love), virtue of
    definition of, 64
    nature of, 63
Church, prayer of, 42–43, 59–61, 107. *see also* Liturgy of Church
church, as place of prayer, 83
communion with God, prayer as, 12, 93, 113
companions, prayer, 78–82
    catechists, 81
    members of religious orders, 81
    ordained ministers, 81
    prayer groups, 81–82
    Saints, 79–80
    spiritual directors, 82, 84
Confirmation, Lord's Prayer in, 107
contemplation
    definition of, 98
    nature of, 81, 93
covenant
    definition of, 14
    prayer as, 12
Covenant of Sinai, 20, 21–22, 26
convent(s), 83
conversation, prayer as, 30

conversion
    definition of, 38
    Jesus' call to, 34
    prayer of, 24, 34
creation, as manifestation of God, 20–21
Cyril of Jerusalem (Saint), 125

D

daily bread, 119–20
daily prayer, 88
David, prayer of the People of God and, 23
"Deliver us from evil," 123
Diaspora
    definition of, 26
    formation of psalms and, 25
Didache, 107, 108
distractions, 94
Divine Office, 83, 84
Divine Providence, 118–20, 124
dryness, 95

E

Elijah, prayer of conversion of, 23–24
Eucharist
    centrality of, to Christian prayer, 42, 88
    Lord's Prayer and, 107
    as prayer of thanksgiving, 49
evil, 123

F

failure to pray, 94
faith
    definition of, 64
    lack of, 96
    nourishing, in times of dryness, 95
    prayer of, 21, 36
    Theological Virtue of, 61
family, Christian, 81
Father. *see* God the Father
"Footprints," 11
"Forgive us our trespasses," 120–22
forgiveness, asking for, 47. *see also* petition, prayer of
Francis of Assisi (Saint), 91, 92

G

Gandhi, 19
gestures, words and, 68
"Give us this day our daily bread," 118–120
God
    presence of, 63, 97, 112–13
    universal search for, 18–19